Quixotic Notions

Quixotic Notions

Poems, Paintings, and Ekphrastic Poetry

Gary D. Swaim

Literary Press
Lamar University

Copyright © 2018 Gary D. Swaim
All Rights Reserved

ISBN: 978-1-942956-59-4
Library of Congress Control Number: 2018954915

Manufactured in the United States of America
Book Design: Theresa L. Ener

Lamar University Literary Press
Beaumont, Texas

Acknowledgments

I am grateful to the editors of the following journals and books for publishing some of the poems or paintings included in this book.

8 Voices, Contemporary Poetry from the American Southwest
Amarillo Bay
Ardent! (featured poet)
Aries
Azusa Pacific University
The Burden of Light: Poems on Illness and Loss
Chest
DFW Poets Anthology
Kalyna Review, of the Ukraine
The Mayo Review
Morris Memorial Chapbook
New Texas
The New Yorker
Penwood Review
A Perhaps Line: Poetry of the Material and Spiritual Worlds
Red River Review
Rider of Asses, chapbook
SWCCL, Baylor
The Whirlwind Review
Windhover

CONTENTS

Poems

- 15 Collecting Pieces
- 16 Be Mindful: We Are Standing on Hallowed Ground
- 17 Bossa Nova
- 18 Divertissement
- 20 So Little to Talk About
- 21 For Kimberly, My Student
- 23 Coma
- 24 A Comatose Poet's Brain Scan
- 26 Colors
- 27 Terza Rima Noir
- 34 Capri
- 35 Marialena's World
- 36 Young Neruda
- 37 For Rev. Daniel Berrigan
- 38 Jake and Janice
- 39 Aubade
- 41 Adam to Eve (I)
- 42 Adam to Eve (II)
- 43 Adam to Eve (III)
- 44 Eve to Adam (I)
- 45 Eve to Adam (II)
- 46 *das Ding an Sich*
- 47 Pantoums for Bathsheba
- 53 Pantoums for David
- 59 For Jeffrey
- 60 Union
- 61 Ekphrastic Poem
- 62 The Door
- 64 The Fall
- 65 Sleep: A Dramatic Dialogue
- 71 A Young Boy's Flight
- 72 Barcarolle
- 73 I Am Well
- 74 Job's Song
- 77 Don't Run
- 78 Andy's Apologia
- 80 Discomfort
- 81 The Birth of Ishmael
- 82 Circumcision (*brit milah*)
- 83 Number Thirteen

84	Were I to Write a Letter
86	Benny and the Gang
88	Eschatology
90	A Professor's Perspective, and . . .
91	Upright Blues in the Key of F
93	Scot Joplin Reminisces
95	Gravity (I)
96	Gravity (II)
97	Exhalations
99	Masks
100	Coda
102	I Have Travelled
104	Daughters, Do Not Weep for Me
106	A Reading
108	Black and White Rag
110	Fugue
113	'Zounds!
114	Nibblings
116	Now or Later?
118	Spoken Words Heal
119	An Old Writer's Interview
144	Ambiguity
146	Laughter
147	Feet

Paintings

cover	Quixote
11	Star Bright Star Light
13	Geometry Dressed for the Dance
17	The Serape
19	Face of Sorrow
20	Waiting
22	Birds
26	A Lightness of Being
33	Shake It Off
34	The Cyclades
37	Through the Gates
39	Shape Shifter Butterfly or Proteus
40	High Desert Flaring Sun
44	Eve's Allure
52	Alexandria, Egypt
58	Where Is Bathsheba?

59	Menorah and the Star of David
63	Open the Door
64	Blind Teiresias
70	Tree Shells Against the Sky
71	Live Wires
77	Birches
79	Footloose
85	Buddhist Prophet in Standing Meditation
87	Trio II
89	Night Feeding
90	Seaman's Leisure Reading
92	Standup Bass Rambler Rattlers
94	Slow Touch on the Keys
98	Egret in Flight
99	Theatre Masks
101	Crosby Stills and Nash
103	Woman's Face Study
105	Crux
107	White Hat
109	Blow!
112	Piano Fortissimo
115	St. Francis and Friends
117	SMU's Dallas Hall
143	Four Horsemen of the Apocalypse
145	Colors of the Spirit
147	Three Is Company
148	Breaking Conformity's Back
149	Afterword

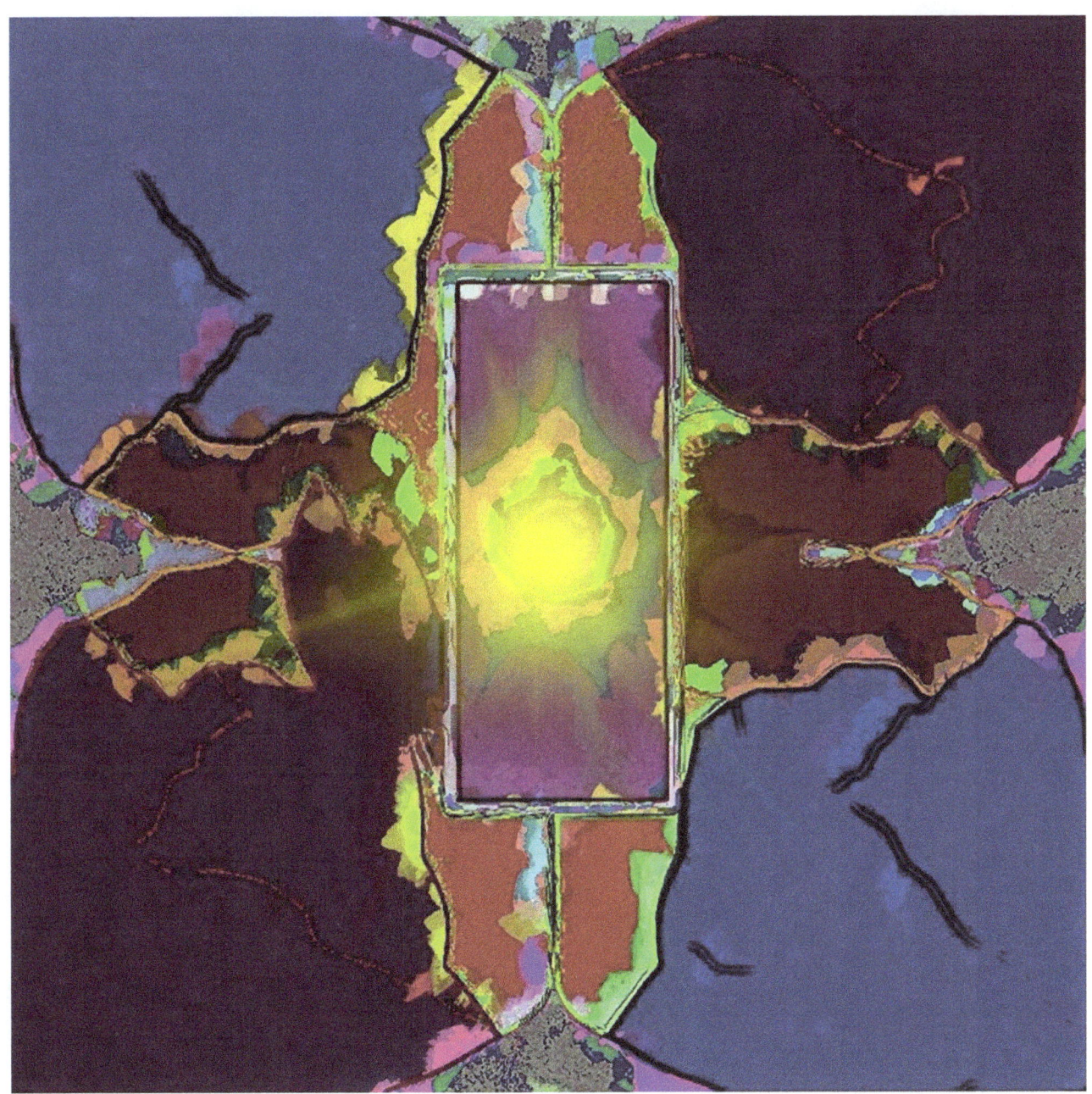

Star Bright Star Light

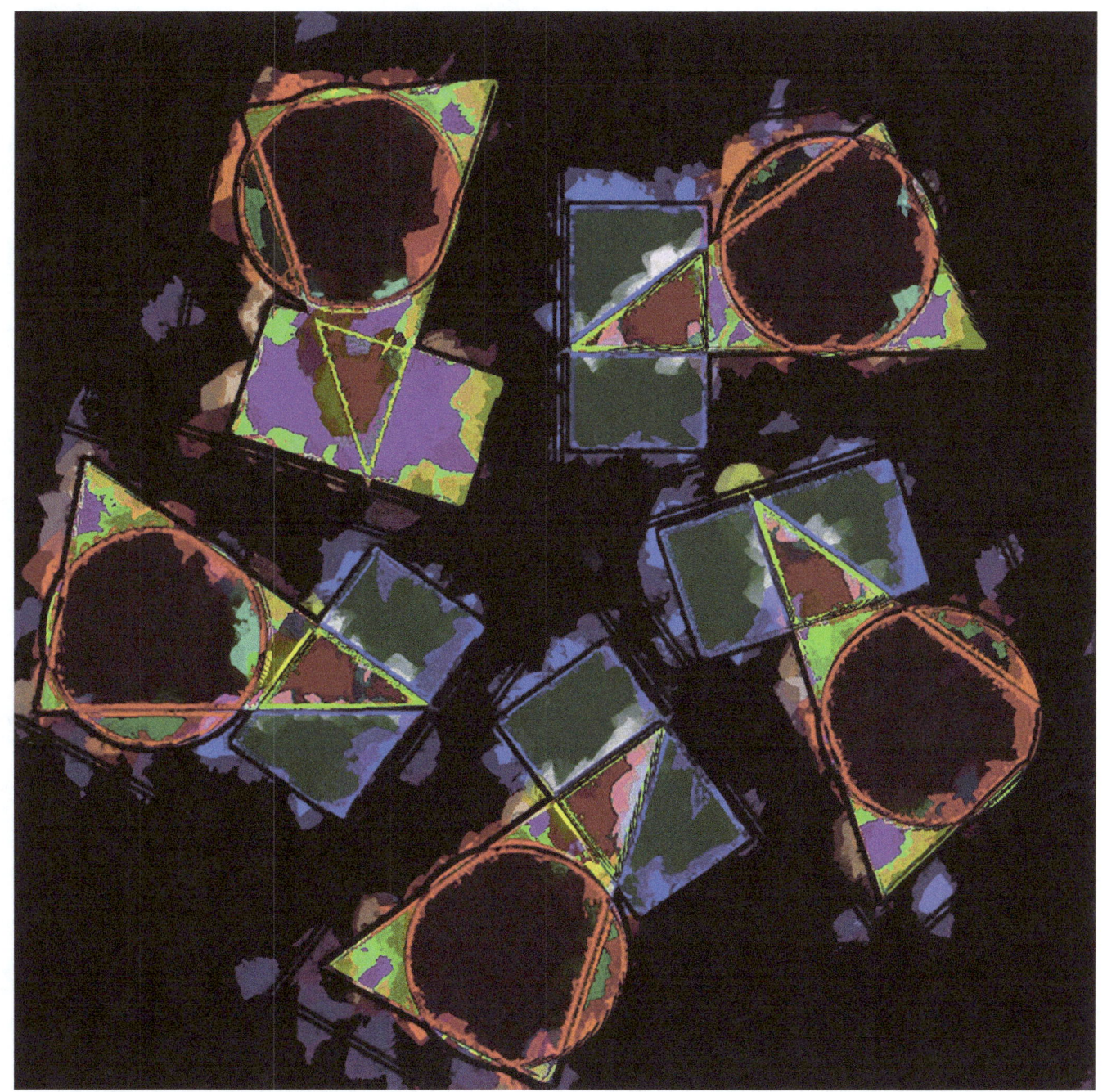
Geometry Dressed for the Dance

Collecting Pieces

Still, at this late age in life, I look
for separate pieces of my soul,

scattered, I believe, like shards
of pottery across the land.

Once I dug in an Italian farmer's field,
in sludge following hard rain, hands

reaching deep into rich, black mud,
bringing up darkened bits of tile

from ancient Roman roofs, even
an Etruscan amphora pot handle.

It's like that, I believe. Were I to find
a shard of my soul here, one there, then

another and another, until every single piece
of who I am fit together, making the whole,

would I, on looking at the assemblage,
be reluctant at being placed on an artful stand,

shown to the world?

Be Mindful: We Are Standing on Hallowed Ground

Where then should I look?
   It is ground, look beneath your feet.
But, as I look there, I see broken shards of dirt.
   So much in our world is fragmented. It was not always so.
Am I capable of repairing it? Is that not too great a task?
   Can you be mindful?

I do not know. What must I do?
   Pay attention.
To what?
   To everything. Everything is broken.
Is that not too much for one person to do? Pay attention to everything?
   Not if you look only beneath your feet shown to the world.

Oh, I see.
   Yes, I believe you do.

Bossa Nova

He gathers her from a metal
chair, cradles her cautiously
in his arms. They dance.

Jobim and Gilberto
know nothing of MS, nor tonight
does she as, with closed eyes buried
deeply in his chest, her mind moves
to slow, complicated rhythms
of the bossa nova while limp legs
trail marionette-like along the polished
floor.

The Serape

Divertissement

Ice on the roadways
biscuits in the pan,
terror in the bone
as I ask him and

wait . . . for a reply.
Non sequitur, all
he gives as I try
to get through that wall,

rip through that grin, that face,
just twist it into place.
"Well, it was late, Love."
All he's got to say,

"Nothing, Turtledove,
just a little play
And, I'd been drinking,
well, a dash too much.

I wasn't thinking . . .
Why not let me touch
you, hold you close to me?
I'm still your guy, you'll see."

The cold in the room
crawls into my veins,
a rancid perfume
assaults my membranes.

I ask once more,
just beneath the breath,
and now can't ignore
the slow smell of death.

I smile—touch of remorse.
"Will you fight a divorce?"

Face of Sorrow

So Little to Talk About

We haven't talked about it. We entered an agreement of silence,
which is fine except when we both hear slow, measured breathing
just above our heads.

If our conversation were an alphabet poem, there would be no letter "c,"
or perhaps the letter "d." Difficult non-conversation. No mention of
chocolate candy, cactus (well, we don't talk about that much anyway),
No caffeine. That's what her doctor said, so we've already stopped that,
too. No, cantaloupe. It's Spring and I'd love to talk about cantaloupe.

"Still dizzy?" No, I can't say that, though she has been of late. I recently
went to my dentist, but now I have to call him the tooth physician, even
with the "c" couched in physician. Can't say dilettante. I've always liked
that word, but you'll not hear me say it again except in this poem. If it's
in a poem, no one will see it anyway.

How can anyone have anything that resembles a conversation? Very
apparent, with all this stumbling about, that I can't.

    I may have cancer.

Waiting

For Kimberly, My Student
—7/29/13

Occasionally, we would walk slowly
to our separate cars after our seminar,
and her mind would dart the evening
skies, reminding me of my childhood
California swallows.

A question here . . . another there.
She had to know. It was important
that she know, anything—everything
she could. Pick up that small piece
of straw, carry it back to her nest.
There was not much time. The sun
raced down, the sky grew darker.

    ****

"Just one more questions, please,"
she would say. "I must build my nest,
make it full. A great darkness is coming."

    ****

And, my answer: "Neither of us will fill
our nests, but know that you will always
seek, find, and radiate small glimmers

of light, my swift friend of flight.
"Fly away now. Find what you can,
and share your discoveries with those
of us who live beneath the moon."

Birds

Coma

So, now I know. How gentle the nightmares of young sleep.
Dark bed coverings may roil restless legs toward two a.m., then four,
perhaps six, especially of a Saturday morning, when one should
be bundled in warmest blankets of sleeping comfort.

But, sapling Sabbath nightmares, even with grand black tarantulas
crawling bedposts and legs and eyelids, have a mildness about them
when compared to what I endure now. I suspend somewhere
(I am not allowed to know where) between some bleak Hadean
universe and the blackness of a vaulting, limitless sky, head convulsing
with each fifteen-minute turn of my rotating, iron lung of a bed,
a sarcophagus if I've ever known one. Head downward an eternal
fifteen, sideways another, then upward where I see only a void.

>No! I see constellations! Andromeda, flaring
>daughter of King Cepheus, Queen Cassiopeia.
>If I must be suspended, let it be here.

And, they turn me sideways, yet again.

It's now as though I see through a slit to those watching: cardiologist, pulmonologist,
attentive nurse or two. Each squeezed into this small cleft through which my glazed
eyes try to touch what my hands cannot. I think my eyes have just shut (I cannot know
for sure. I know so little) . . . blinked perhaps for attention.

They don't see me, and am turned again.
>So it goes, interminably.

An ICU Ferris wheel, for the dying. Let the thin voice of Calliope
sing me into the deepest of all slumbers.

A Comatose Poet's Brain Scan

"It's fifty days now, Doctor.
Not even the flutter of an eyelash."

    "Linda, please! You can do better
    than a languid, limping cliché. Reach!
    Give the Doctor something more desperate.
    'Iamb' in here, however still I may be.
    Grab him by the throat with your metaphors:
    He has lain in my grandfather's grave for days now.
    See?"

        "We're doing all we can, Linda. Second MRI
        this time. We really think he's dying."

"Dying! Doc, I've got at least a chapbook
of poems doing somersaults in this head
you're doing radioactive assaults on. Watch
my lips. My lips are moving, aren't they?"

        "Not even his lips have moved. We sometimes
        see, at least, that. One hopeful sign to look for, Linda."

"I could swear they moved. Alright, now. Watch this!"

        "See? Nothing. It's like watching grass grow, but it doesn't. There's really nothing else
        we can do."

"Okay, I'll turn flips for you, if that's what it takes.
Let me get my legs untangled first. They're like some
jingle-jangle paragraphs written by freshmen on their
first exam. Everything's twisted. Don't you think they
look like some big, soft pretzel? Hear the organ grinder?
Are you guys blind and deaf?"

        "I've haven't seen such straight, pale, emaciated legs like that since the cadavers we
        worked on in med school. We need to start shutting things down, Nurse. Not even his
        lips have moved. We sometimes see, at least that. One hopeful sign to look for.

"Wait! Wait! One last try on that little toe on my
right foot. There! See? You can see it now, can't you?

"Look, Doctor! Did you see that? That small phalange moved, right foot. I swear it did." "It did! Dear God, it did?"

"No end-stopped line here, just a momentary caesura."

Colors

Lighting on bright thistles, aster, and joe-pye weed
a diminutive Painted Lady thrusts an even brasher color
on her world. A flash of orange against prickly reds and purples.
Morning incandescence unmatched at the sun's rising.

Though its flamboyant orange you first see, mistaking the black
bruise-looking patches for dark leaves on which she rests,
the light of clearer day shows murky colors mottled with bright—
fearsome beauty.

Someone has said dark stains streaking the butterfly's wings
come from the male's violent love making and serve as weights to keep
his Painted Lady from flying away.

A Lightness of Being

Terza Rima Noir

I put a 45 on the table at my side.
Close my eyes to get a wink or two.
Nothing keeps a guy up like thoughts of homicide.

I'm in a rented Armani—dark, dark blue,
Hung over, too many shots, bad scotch.
Both temples in my head feel tips of screws

Snaking paths into my eyes that can't watch
Any longer for the blokes on London shore
Intent on squeezing the balls in my crotch.

Fog slithers in like some one-night whore,
Dressed in street-light yellow and deep shades of brown.
All I see are dreams of a stevedore

Standing on a dock then falling into water, down
Into the Thames 'long side Aldergate Street.
Tumble down, tumble down. Down, down, down.

Six o-clock in the AM, world seems brighter.
My eyelids open to the rising of the sun.
All I can think is "I need a barrister,"

Get me outa this fix.
I put my hand on the table,
Slowly slip the 45 in. "Naah, nix,"

I just can't, so I pick up an empty glass
Feel the warmth in my cold hand.
"What I need's *two* barristers to cover my ass."

I straighten my tie, put the left shoe on,
Squint at the sun rising through the blinds.
Feel the presence of the squirming gun.

I start at the sudden knock on the door,
Move cautiously from my chair to the room's other side.
Hand on the knob, both feet on the floor,
I look through the keyhole to the other side,

Breathe with relief at what I see.
She's walking away. I now see her backside

Swinging to and fro in a bright orange swish
Rippling like a river on its way to the sea
"God! She's some extraordinary, fine dish."

He jerks the door quickly, opens it wide,
Calls to her backside now down the hall.
"Hey, Babe, you've got some kinda glide

"Like a smooth, slim craft that's just been launched
And's headed East to the far Azores.
How's 'bout comin' back? I've got a hunch

You were looking for me. Promise not to bore
You too much with questions multitudinous.
Just love to see both the aft and the fore.

Three-quarters down the hallway she spins, a bit mutinous
Then spits out a phrase he'd never forget.
"I'm not your easy, sail-by-night nautilus.

"Neither am I some marionette
Looking for someone to pull my strings.
My name's Lorainne Claudette."

Finally . . . at last . . . he'd met his match
And squirmed with delight at this stunning sight,
He knew he had managed a prize catch.

"Mind if I call you Claudette? That's the one I like."
"Call me anything you want to call me.
Not much in this world I dislike."

Jake liked the attitude, and he could see
That she had some brights on her fore and in her head.
She approached him with a step, then gave him a knee

In the balls where it hurts like hell, legs outspread
He muffled a cry, then went to the floor,
Face turned blue, then orange, then red.

"What'd ya do that for?" And then he swore,
"Damn it to hell, I was just bein' nice.
Get me through this freakin' door!

My scrotum feels like it's in some kind of vice.
What'd you *do* that for?
I was just bein' nice."

Claudette picked him off the walnut floor,
Dusted him off, walked him to the bed.
He didn't feel at *this* moment so cocksure.

Forget the cock, and he tried . . . tried instead
To think about this lethal blonde in front of his eyes.
He slowly thought he might have misled

Her with his cocky . . . forget cocky . . . his high-
Flown vocabulary out of Roget's Thesaurus.
Naah, it had to be something else she heard him imply.

* * *

Jake woke up, an anvil in his head and a few clouds, cumulus
Loads of bad scotch and a knee to the balls
That's all he could remember. My God, who was she, Succubus?

He felt for a pulse, heard a thump. Alcohol,
He thought, running headlong to his brain.
He rolled to the floor and began to crawl

To the ramshackle window, looked at the pane,
Climbed to the sill, raised the blinds slowly
Oh, dear God, the pain.

He faced a stunning light—shocked wholly
By a piercing glare from the sun
He thought of the Isles of Stromboli

Where volcanoes shot basalt by the ton
With glaring bright lights toward Sicily, his love,
Then he shut his eyes, completely undone.

He slumped to the floor again, opened his eyes, looked above
Then looked around the room for his gun

Saw it six feet away, over by the stove.

Then his brain stirred. He remembered someone
Who had made a quite pleasing impression.
Jake saw her clearly and became surprisingly undone.

Orange chiffon and the face of a bright, young nun.
He was always taken aback by the Church
Where his first sexual adventures had begun.

Claudette! He knew he was on a fresh search.
Forget the stevedore, at least for the moment.
If he could get up, he thought. First things first.

    * * *

Jake walks down the street with the trace of a limp
Still feeling the pain in one of his balls.
His gait made him look like some street pimp

But he pushed on down the way, a block at a time
And all he could see was orange chiffon and some lace.
His thoughts sneaked up, almost a crime.

Then he spotted two guys in black Burberry coats
Carrying heat just under their left arms.
All of a sudden a catch in his throat.

These weren't no frat boys with hootch under their arms.
They were the Limeys his nightmares were about.
Clearly, he thought, they're on the prowl for more harm.

He tucked his head and buried his snout,
Picked up his pace, could hear the click of his heels
As he got closer he *knew*, there could be no doubt.

These were the guys, then he suddenly wheeled
In the other direction, he thought it was East.
Yeah, gotta get outa here. That's the deal,

Otherwise they'll see me, remember me, at the least.
Not now! Can't let that happen, not right now.
Gotta get outa here, walk fast on the lam, Bernice!

Head to St. Jonathan's. Find Joe the Priest,
Tell him all my issues,
Confess to him everything, the whole story, complete.

                          * * *

"You see, it's this way, Father," he said through the scrim.
"I saw this guy mauled then thrown into the Thames,
It was a pitch black night, man (I mean Father), it was grim.

"I could see these guys' faces. And they got a glimpse
Of my puss and came runnin' on a trot.
At first, I couldn't think, so I just froze. I mean every limb.

Then, I ran like a thoroughbred. Legs seemed tied in a knot.
But, I ran into the dark just far enough away
For them to miss me. I squatted down and thought a lot

About what to do next. How'd I get caught in this fray?
I just don't have a clue which way to turn.
I don't have a clue what to say

To anyone. Guess I won't ever learn.
I'm scared shitless, Father. Sorry, that word wasn't called for,
But my stomach don't do nothin' but churn.

I was thinkin' of you, on the streets, just a bit ago.
I'm needing to ask you for some help, of any sort.
Is there anything you can do, you know . . .

Tell the Bobbies, you know, file a report
About what a friend of yours saw?
I don't mean to be some slimy wart

That snitches on something, something stuck in his craw,
But this is important. I know you agree.
Someone, not me's, gotta tell 'em what I saw."

Jake listened to the silence. He needed to pee.
The priest shuffled quietly then ultimately said,
With a solemn voice to his lackluster devotee,

"Jake, young man, I've known you forever. Something's unsaid.
Tell me all, and I'll see what I can do."

Jake's shoulders fell like a lump of lead.

And after another long silence, Jake finally knew—
"Father, I've sinned. Everything I've told you is a bald faced lie.
I'm in the middle of this thing like some bug in glue.

What can I say? A thousand hail Mary's? Will that nullify
My sins, really? Will it take off this load
Weighting me down? Yeah, I shot the guy,

He fell in the water, down, down, down. A toad's
What he was. Ripped me off for a thousand bucks.
That's the end of that bad episode.

End of me, too, the epitome of bad luck.
Lost little orange Claudette. My!
Sometimes, life just sucks.

What you gonna do now, Father? I've told you all that's true.
Gonna throw me up against the wall? Make sure I'll never see orange again?
Yeah, well . . . to little orange Claudette I didn't get to know, I bid adieu."

Shake It Off

Capri

In some ages past, Neolithic time perhaps, God wrapped a
piece of what we now call Italy in His hand, curled His fingers
about it with capricious care, and in what would seem a violent act,
tore Capri, like a thin sheet of papyrus, from its original home.

Craggy, chalk-like cliff sides devoid, one would guess, of life
but destined to be aswarmed with greenery on which God
could rest following days of labor. Shocking flowers encircled
Him with their beauty, and He said, "It is good, oh, so very good

by the edge of the Tryrrhean Sea." And, it would be good, so very good
for thousands upon thousands of tourists, then residents: August Caesar
for his summer home, writers Rilke and Gorky, other writers, artists
and dancers, performing their crafts to the rhythms of the dark blue waters

of the *Gratta Azzurra*.

The Cyclades

Marialena's World

I don't know Marialena.
I know only her love.
Lying here immobile, I know
it is she at the door. Even before
her slight voice, a sumptuous Italian
perfume wafts beneath the door sill
just as her delicate left hand appears.

It is Tuesday, and I am in Tuscany.
I smell tall green pines swishing
almost imperceptibly to a warm southern
breeze, threaded with a light Orvieto Chianti
aroma. She steps close and extends her right hand,
touching my stolid arm and from her comes a breath
of pineapple Italian gelati. I inhale her and from my bed
see Petrarch in dark candlelight writing a sonnet.

It's Wednesday, perhaps; an early morning Adriatic Sea spray
is her aroma. I'm in Capri, riding the rail up to Anacapri,
now at the cliff's edge—where Rilke looked down on Tiberius'
summer home and penned words this poet can never match.
My mind rushes with his swift pen: "The rose is a distilling
eye. It gathers light and filters it until the concentration is
powerful and pure. . . ." Little light in this white room,
only a flowering red I see rising about Marialena's lips.

Is it Thursday or Friday? Something raw, musky in Marialena's aroma
as she lifts her arms at the door to slide the yellow plastic from her body
and again approach my bed. Now also absent the yellow gloves, her naked index finger touches my
bare shoulder as if to awaken me. I've been awake hours. I catch just a whiff of another of the
perfumes she loves. I am in Rome

                               and know I am better now.

Young Neruda

No more than eight or ten, slogging through Chilean forests
water to his knees, just below the cut of his short britches
insects, unnamed colors, small and gargantuan slay at bare skin
of his arms, legs, and face, even crawl through his hair.
Still, he moves slowly, this dancer among trees and water
and abundant life, when he extends a hand, cups small
fingers about a soft-shelled living thing he has never seen
before, brings it close to his steady eyes (the observer)
places it, after time on the tiniest of his fingers and brings
it to his lips, giving it the lightest of kisses (the lover).
    He almost whispers, "My first poem."

For Rev. Daniel Berrigan

Oh, Daniel—brave, righteous law breaker, rest in peace.
Beat swords into plowshares in your dreams, heavy
submachine guns to children's Zephyr bicycles. Dream
us into peace, with Jesuit knowledge that dreams mean
nothing.

Your efforts were feckless, noble. Slashing blades,
hot metaled guns press against our throats, still. It
will always be so. Human blood runs through our veins.
You sought, challengingly, to infuse veins with vapors
from the Spirit. Still we are left languid, bereft of Holiness,
types O, A, B, and admixtures converging on sands and streets.

Through the Gates

Jake and Janice

Jake lived by fifths: Wild Turkey, Jamison, Old Bushmill.
Janice by teaspoons: Splenda, vanilla, and just a touch of half and half.

Mix whiskey or scotch with dribbles of anything but clear,
pure water and, in time, the taste turns bitter.

After only a year, Jake and Janice fell into liquid pools
of despair, their palates for one another no longer manageable.

Shape Shifter Butterfly or Proteus

Aubade

> *"Early the next morning Abraham took some food and a skin of water and gave them to Hagar. He set them on her shoulders and then sent her off with the boy. She went on her way and wandered in the desert of Beersheba."* Genesis 21:14

Above Beersheba Ishmael cries
and I, doing Jaweh's service, fly
to Him so as to mollify

the young lad's distress,
spend some time at his side, assess
his needs and perhaps dispossess

him of his thoughts for a woeful destiny.
Then, I see a site, devoid of water, so foreign to me
I think it a facsimile

of Mephistopheles' fallen place:
scathing evening heat, wholly lacking grace.
I've never seen surroundings quite so base.

My wings shudder in grit and sand
that grinds into them over this godforsaken land
and I wonder why I joined my hymn-singing, angelic band.

Wonder, too, if these wings will ever again be white
or if I can explain to Michael this feathery blight,
pinions turned deep reddish-brown, like desert anthracite.

Not certain I'll be much help to Jaweh's forgotten child.
Such an unseemly place: arid, barren—so wild
one would think it fit for only the defiled.

Nearing sunrise now— hard to believe, but so.
Long night's over and there's a beginning glow
in the East where the Judean Mountains form an intaglio

against the horizon, a gleaming bronze jewel
and in the foreground I see the barest outline of a new pool
of water, there where Hagar sleeps as the night unspools.

She's sleeping a bowshot's distance from him
for fear she might see him die. She thinks it Jaweh's whim
that Ishmael must lie crying, eyes now dim.

The sun rises above a far mountain peak.
Hagar rises, too, with painful stretches of her limbs, weak
and spies a fountain she's not seen before by a fresh desert creek.

She moves in morning pain to a now glistening well
carrying an animal skin to hold life's water. She will tell Ishmael,
at my urging, that Jaweh from this early morning's pastel

skies has dropped blessings on them, that they will live and flourish
in new lands, perhaps the wondrous desert of Paran, and his wish
to become a brave archer will be satisfied—no need for anguish.

It's most in early morning hours that Jaweh demonstrates how wise
He is. Falling dew, gentle breezes, hues of red and orange epitomize
His wisdom. Beersheba—a lovely land? Jaweh's dawning surprise.

High Desert Flaring Sun

Adam to Eve (I)

My lips tasted pungent fruit as I watched
you rise from my side, limb by limb. Every step

a liquid movement like Euphrates' waters
flowing through our garden.

I lay still, for fear of my gaping wound,
fear, too, that I might startle and set astonishing

motions in your body, driving you to the edge
of Eden. You took but a few steps eastward,

turned back to me, creased a smile, and sweet smells
from a distant tree told me you would not leave.

Adam to Eve (II)

Wholly drawn to you newly from my side,
I watch your languid motions and wonder
what compels me so. It feels like thunder
sounds, running through my bones like some great tide.

My body changes—strangeness, I confide.
Frighteningly new. I think, "To win her
like some toy, what must I do? To hold her,
call her mine, turn her here and there in pride."

Then, you move, not some bauble's moves, a dancer's.
Assured, light, coming toward me, I fear.
You brush my arm, I move to grasp you—tight,
but I am weak, a plaything's your answer
and you are right, a plaything to have near,
to reach for that fruit there up at its height.

Adam to Eve (III)

Our bodies fall to the ground beneath us,
limbs tangling in awkward, lustful turns.
I fumble with what you call breasts. I must
learn what this is we do, this act that burns.
I seem all angles abrupt—hard, straight lines.
You are swirls and curves, soft surprising twists.
We do our strange geometry, I mine,
you yours, having learned what we call a kiss.
What is this strangeness we do? It excites
my body, jars my mind. My time is spent,
waking and sleeping, with just how we might
love the next time. Is this why you were sent?
To slake my ever rising appetite?
I'll wait for you beneath His tree tonight.

Eve to Adam (I)

I stepped from your side wearing those red stiletto
heels your gonads demand, feet sharing the ache

of your body's wound. Your eyes, varnished with desire,
Adam, reflected my breasts.

I turned away, felt a vitrifying heat in the stare coating each
crease, each curve of my backside.

Is this why I'm here, to be ogled through that spyglass
hanging between your legs?

I'll walk to the east a bit, try to calm myself, perhaps
pick some fruit for your damned dinner tonight.

Eve's Allure

Eve to Adam (II)

Looking at you lying there on the ground,
I have to ask if God cares one fig for me.
Long past what you call thunder (I call orgasmic twitch),
you lounge there, late-night debauchee.

Get up off your haunches, Adam!
I'm tired of pruning hedges to the tune of your profundities.
God's told us to name animals
and you lie there like some pink anemone.

There's a name, fits *you* very well
planted there in that spot for, well, gee,
who knows how long. I noticed today a strange slithering
thing, Adam, by that tall, stunning and fruited tree.

It moves with a cheeky grace and power.
I think I'll give it a name, let's see—
Adam, have you heard a word I've said?
Adam! Adam! How do you like the name Destiny?

das Ding an Sich

Throw it on out with that deep-throated bellow
of yours. You say you have all the answers.
Give me that low-church glossolalia or that
high-church Aramaic, Greek, or Hebrew.
Read word for word the songs of John
or Solomon. Tell me the rational precision
you find there.

You never touch *das Ding an Sich*.
Your interpretations, your many slip-and-slide
tongues make your world overly wearied,
damned to a place you are certain you can
describe. Go ahead. Try Sanskrit, if that's
your choice. It won't get you much either.
You're reduced to stumbling silence
        as am I and all others.

Pantoums for Bathsheba

Childhood:
It seems I know so much of you, Bathsheba, and so little.
Were both your Mother and Father Hittites, the homeless, say the Israelites?
Weren't these the people that did not exist until the 19th century,
When archaeologists found pieces of your empire throughout the Middle-East?

Were both your Mother and Father Hittites, the homeless, say the Israelites?
Did your family live in a hovel? Was your home uncovered
When archaeologists found pieces of your empire throughout the Middle-East?
Perhaps you lived in a Donald Trump home, wanting nothing for comfort.

Did your Mother and Father love you as most parents love their children?
Perhaps you lived in a Donald Trump home, wanting nothing for comfort,
Except the love you futilely sought.
Did your Mother and Father love you as most parents love their children?

This is not an unimportant question. You may have been given lavish gifts,
Designer clothing and the like, everything except the love you futilely sought.
What are the truths of your childhood?
Did your Mother and Father really love you?

Anatolia:
Did the whole of your household, Bathsheba, worship the goddess,
A vulture priestess with human legs?
Did a fabric hang from your wall with painted eggs and butterflies inside,
The fearsome vulture, tearing at the heads of humans?

A vulture priestess with human legs
Flying in the face of Yaweh?
And yet, I am told, She gives birth, protects, and resurrects.
What more might one ask of a god?

Flying in the face of Yaweh?
Is She not in your culture the Yaweh of Israel?
What more might one ask of a god?
I ask for no more: birth, protection, and resurrection.

Is She not in your culture,
Horrid though She may appear?
I ask for no more.
My Yaweh, the Yaweh of Israel, has no face.

Geography:
Aren't your people those who did not exist?
The Land of Hatti, assimilating Turkey and Syria?
The Children of Heth?
Mesopotamia?

The Land of Hatti, assimilating Turkey and Syria.
How would the Hittites view their world of today?
Mesopotamia?
A pot boiler of rebellions. Perhaps so.

How would the Hittites view their world of today?
Iraq, Afghanistan, perhaps Iran—Syria, Turkey?
A pot boiler of rebellions. Perhaps so.
But it's the geography of your soul I want to know, Bathsheba.

Iraq, Afghanistan, perhaps Iran—Syria, Turkey?
Pot boilers, I'm sure that must be so.
But it's the geography of your soul I want to know, Bathsheba.
I'll know, I'm sure, only if I look at mine.

Bathing:
Did you know King David was watching as you bathed?
Did you know he paced his rooftop, a vulture King at that moment?
But neither birth nor protection was on his mind.
It was you he thought of, you for whom he lusted.

Did you know he paced his rooftop, a vulture King at that moment?
He knew what he would do. Did you know he was attending to you?
It was you he thought of, you for whom he lusted.
Did you drop your Victoria's Secret opalescent teddy to the ground?

He knew what he would do. Did you know he was attending to you?
Did you seduce this King, this man after God's own heart?
Did you drop your Victoria's Secret opalescent teddy to the ground?
You knew it heightened the beauty of your dark skin, didn't you?

Did you seduce this King, this man after God's own heart?
Or was it simply he, being what men can be?
You knew it heightened the beauty of your dark skin, didn't you?
Now what will you do?

Uriah:
He was a good man, this Uriah the Hittite.
It seems I know more of him than I know of you, Bathsheba.
He must have loved you and the King he served, David.
He fought the Ammonites with all of Israel, as the King watched you bathe.

It seems I know more of him than I know of you, Bathsheba.
"Go and kill all the Ammonites." — "Yes, Sir."
He fought the Ammonites with all of Israel, as the King watched you bathe.
I wonder if he believed Anatolia would resurrect those he slew.

"Go and kill all the Ammonites." — "Yes, Sir."
Can any man who kills so easily be called good?
I wonder if he believed Anatolia would resurrect those he slew.
I can only hope so.

Can any man who kills so easily be called good?
Did he make love to you with gentleness?
I can only hope so.
I would hope Uriah sought some gentleness in a world of savagery.

The Assignation:
You were home when there was a knock at your door.
Did you quickly grab a garb and throw it about yourself to answer?
It was, of course, one of King David's servants.
Was there hesitancy at the request of you to join King David?

Did you quickly grab a garb and throw it about yourself to answer?
Surely a modesty would demand at least that.
Was there hesitancy at his request of you to join King David?
Did you, at first, refuse the offer?

Surely a modesty would demand at least that.
But you gathered your necessaries quickly in the absence of Uriah.
Did you, at first, refuse the offer?
I would guess not.

But you gathered your necessaries quickly in the absence of Uriah.
You walked on cobble-stone streets, sandals clicking. A mare in heat.
I would guess not,
Yet, couldn't you have refused the advance?

The Bed:
You lay with the glaze of your body covering a part of the bed like silken cover,
King David's bare body already showing sharp, manly angles.
The dark of your skin suggested evening desert sands with their swirling curves.
His hands gently coursed the whole of your luxuriant body.

King David's bare body already showing sharp, manly angles
Lay softly on yours.
His hands gently coursed the whole of your luxuriant body.
Then, thrusts. One would not know they could be so gentle.

Lay softly on yours?
Had Uriah ever been so moderate?
Then, thrusts. One would not know they could be so gentle.
Will you miss your husband, Uriah?

Had Uriah ever been so moderate? You know, do you not,
that he is killing for his King?
Will you miss your husband, Uriah?
He'll soon be dead at the hand of your lover.

Repercussions:
It was because of you and your lover that Yaweh was displeased.
You gave birth to a son upon becoming King David's wife.
The child would not live.
The God of Israel lay bare His anger.

You gave birth to a son upon becoming King David's wife.
Could you have expected no repercussions?
The God of Israel lay bare His anger.
David fasted and fell distraught upon the earth.

Could you have expected no repercussions?
The child lay ill, deathly so.
David fasted and fell distraught upon the earth.
Servants sought to soothe their King's grief. He'd have none of it.

The child lay ill, deathly so,
When David's servants began to whisper sadly.
Servants sought to soothe their King's grief. He'd have none of it
Yet, the child died, and King David suffered Yaweh's wrath.

Anointment:
Your saucy lover, now husband, Bathsheba, anointed himself in grief.
Oils of spikenard, myrrh, Rose of Sharon, and Lily of the Valley.
After washing the whole of his body.
He worshipped his God.

Oils of spikenard, myrrh, Rose of Sharon, and Lily of the Valley.
These wouldn't take away his guilt,
He, then, worshipped his God.
There is more to come.

These would not take away his guilt.
Yaweh said, "Because you have despised me and taken the wife of Uriah,
There is more to come.
I will bring evil against you from within your house."

Yaweh said, "Because you have despised me and taken the wife of Uriah,
I will take all your wives and give them to your neighbors.
I will bring evil against you from within your house,
And each wife will lie with a man naked in the sun."

Sorrow Now:
Bathsheba, had you known all these things, would you have lain with David?
Is remorse a word your lips can't speak?
Are those lips only for caresses?
Can you now see what you have done?

Is remorse a word your lips can't speak?
Do you feast now on a Queen's possessions?
Are those lips only for caresses?
I feel sorrow for you, as I feel shudders of disquiet.

Do you feast now on a Queen's possessions?
Perhaps you feel a certain titillation at the absence of other wives.
I feel sorrow for you, as I feel shudders of disquiet.
Was the beginning of all this only a game?

Perhaps you feel a certain titillation at the absence of other wives.
No matter that they lie in sunlit streets, ravaged by men of disgrace.
Was the beginning of all this only a game?
If chess, you would have known the King is always your superior.

Alexandria, Egypt

Pantoums for David

Every Man:
You were not Everyman, David, as was the faithful pawn, mythological Job.
You may, however, be every man with all you did in your storied life.
Job would have served well as one of your pawns, but Bathsheba's door?

No, he would not have knocked on her door.
You may, however, be every man with all you did in your storied life,
Taking Bathsheba to your bed, even if in gentleness?
No, he would not have knocked on her door.

Such an act would have turned his mythological stomach.
Taking Bathsheba to your bed, even if in gentleness, brought
The death of Uriah, for which you must take full responsibility,
Such an act would have turned Job's mythological stomach.

You did what every man might do, not what Job would do.
The death of Uriah, for which you must take full responsibility,
Gnaws at a man like Job.
Your story doesn't begin here, however, does it, David?

Chosen:
Youngest among eight sons of Jesse, the Bethlehemite,
A man of comeliness, enough to create problems, in time.
Anointed festively by Samuel, later self-anointed in grief.
Harpist who calmed the uneasy nerves of his king, Saul.

A man of comeliness, enough to create problems, in time.
Would you live the life you lived, all over again, had you the choice, David?
Harpist who calmed the uneasy nerves of his king, Saul.
Who calmed your nerves, David, player of harps?

Would you live the life you lived, all over again, had you the choice, David?
There are so many things you did, with pride, it seems.
Who calmed your nerves, David, player of harps,
Slayer of thousands upon thousands of those you called enemies?

There are so many things you did, with pride, it seems.
Why did you take the lives of so many?
Slayer of thousands upon thousands of those you called enemies.
What does this say of you, David, "man after God's own heart"—of your Jaweh?

Goliath:
It all started heroically, I mean your real beginning, David.
The Philistines gathered on one mountain top, the Israelites on another,
With a wide valley between, separating them.
Have you forgotten this first battle of the many you waged, David?

The Philistines gathered on one mountain top, the Israelites on another.
The valley between them soon became a plain of streaming blood.
Have you forgotten this first battle of the many you waged, David?
It seems quite possible.

The valley between them soon became a plain of streaming blood.
Ultimately, one band could not defeat the other, so two men would fight.
It seems quite possible.
Nearing nine feet, two inches, covered in brass and iron mail, stood Goliath.

Ultimately, one band could not defeat the other, so two men would fight.
It was you, David, who would kill for the Israelites this day.
Nearing nine feet, two inches, covered in brass and iron mail, stood Goliath
Who would fall with a stone thrown between his eyes by a young warrior.

Jealousy:
Your King Saul used you as a pawn, David. Surely, you knew,
You who would later be hedged about by your own pawns, even a queen.
To the front lines, my comely warrior.
Kill every Philistine who crosses your path, even children who scurry playfully.

You who would later be hedged about by your own pawns, even a queen.
It was you who had beheaded the gargantuan Philistine, Goliath.
"Kill every Philistine who crosses your path, even children who scurry playfully.
Then return in safety to my Rook," says Saul.

It was you who had beheaded the gargantuan Philistine, Goliath.
A bit of irony here, don't you think?
"Return in safety to my Rook," says Saul.
Your safety lasted a short number of days.

A bit of irony here, don't you think?
All of Judah loved you too much, David.
Your safety lasted a short number of days.
Loyal warrior, let this be a lesson in Politics 101 for future days.

Flight:
So many of your days will be spent in flight.
There's no safety among those who ache for dominance.
Hiding in fields, fleeing even to Gath where you had killed Goliath.
Did anger swallow you in escape?

There's no safety among those who ache for dominance.
So, you feigned madness among those of Gath.
Did anger swallow you in escape,
You who allowed spittle to run down your beard, and scratched at gate doors?

So, you feigned madness among those of Gath,
And, again, you fled, living in caves,
You who allowed spittle to run down your beard, and scratched at gate doors. Would there be no place to hide?

And, again, you fled, living in caves.
How dark must those caves have been.
Would there be no place to hide?
Only as one turns his face to Yaweh.

Caves:
It must have been darker than pitch.
How deeply did you go in those cavernous makeshift homes?
Lighted by fire-struck twigs of sticks.
Could you write poetry? Did you sing?

How deeply did you go in those cavernous makeshift homes?
Did desert sandstone caverns allow warmth at night?
Could you write poetry? Did you sing?
How lonely you must have been.

Did desert sandstone caverns allow warmth at night?
I think of the Psalms, many of which I am told, you wrote.
How lonely you must have been.
I recall most the Second Psalm.

I think of the Psalms, many of which I am told, you wrote.
Did you sing them out in hollows of the earth, as you wrote?

I recall most the Second Psalm.
Men of the earth fly recklessly at you in the night.

Second Psalm:
"Why do the heathen rage, and the people imagine a vain thing?"
Did you sing this, David, from one of your caves with a Middle-Eastern trill?
Why do they rage? you ask. Because you have killed indiscriminately.
Philistines, Geshurites, Gezrites, Amalekites, Moabites, Hittites, Ammonites.

Did you sing this, David, from one of your caves, with a Middle-Eastern trill?
The harp seems the wrong instrument for such a song.
Philistines, Geshurites, Gezrites, Amalekites, Moabites, Hittites, Ammonites.
They all hated you, and you them. They were heathen to you.

The harp seems the wrong instrument for such a song.
Rage? Vain speculations? "Saul killed thousands, David, tens of thousands."
They all hated you, and you them. They were heathen to you.
Could you not have seen them differently as we do "so well today?"

Rage? Vain speculations? "Saul killed thousands, David, tens of thousands."
"The kings of the earth set themselves, and the rulers take counsel together."
They all hated you, and you them. They were heathen to you.
Was your Psalm in a fitting minor mode, 4/4 dirge-like time?

Psalms:
"The Kings of the earth set themselves, and the rulers take counsel together
Against the Lord, and against his anointed . . ."
These are your words, they say, written and sung without a harp this day.
My imagination hears the sonority of the harp against stone walls.

"Against the Lord, and against his anointed . . ."
Perhaps you strapped a small harp across your back like a Fender guitar.
My imagination hears the sonority of the harp against stone walls.
It was important, and you carried it wherever you went, strange warrior.

Perhaps you strapped a small harp across your back like a Fender guitar.
The grace of your voice, the lyricism of your words, and the harp.
It was important, and you carried it wherever you went, feral warrior,
With your sword and a knife strapped to your leg.

The grace of your voice, the lyricism of your words, and the harp.
They must have eased your loneliness, especially the harp,

With your sword and a knife strapped to your leg.
Can devices of beauty and horror subsist together?

A Battle:
You reigned over Judah seven years and six months,
Over all of Israel thirty-three years, sharp stone slinger.
Wasting no time, you chose concubines and wives from Jerusalem,
Never far from Bathsheba.

Over all of Israel thirty-three years, sharp stone slinger.
A long way from the Gathian Goliath and your men at war.
Never far from Bathsheba.
Were you watching out for Ammonites while walking your rooftop?

A long way from the Gathian Goliath and your men at war.
Close by, bathed a new woman you wanted. And you watched.
Were you watching out for Ammonites while walking your rooftop?
Only your men fought in the front line. You battled with lust.

Close by, bathed a new woman you wanted. And you watched.
You would not turn your eyes from the dark beauty.
Only your men fought in the front line. You battled with lust.
And, lust, as among many men, won.

Last Things:
Difficult to imagine, you, David, and Bathsheba in old age.
As you lay in your death bed, David, did you remember Bathsheba's dark skin?
Did your name, meaning Beloved, cause you to ask, "By whom?"
Did Bathsheba's request that your son Solomon be anointed King swallow hard?

As you lay in your death bed, David, did you remember Bathsheba's dark skin?
Did you once doubt that you were a man after God's own heart?
Did Bathsheba's request that your son Solomon be anointed King swallow hard?
Could Solomon's wisdom emanate from the two of you?

Did you once doubt that you were a man after God's own heart?
With all you killed, the seduction and compliance, the murder of Uriah,
Could Solomon's wisdom emanate from the two of you?
It is so hard to accept.

With all you killed, the seduction and compliance, the murder of Uriah.
I must conclude, Jaweh looks more to intentions than acts of bizarre humanity.
It is so hard to accept.
Perhaps God weighs aims more than daily, even yearly acts. Perhaps.

Where Is Bathsheba?

For Jeffrey
    (On the Death of my Student—7/11/09)

I am not his father.
He *is* my son.
When we played together,
It was not with toy guns or footballs,
Rather, with syllables, rhythmic patterns,
Iambs, dactyls, end-stopped lines.

Jeffrey, the line of your life should not have stopped.
But, then, perhaps no lifeline should or does.
Let's suppose, if only for great fun, that we all roll about in sonnets
And villanelles with Shakespeare and Dylan Thomas,
Or the free verse of a Whitman or Galway Kinnell,
That we are then free from that which pulls us down, down . . .
Into a deep well, surfeited with sorrow, that we are instead, the poem,
Giving joy to the reader.

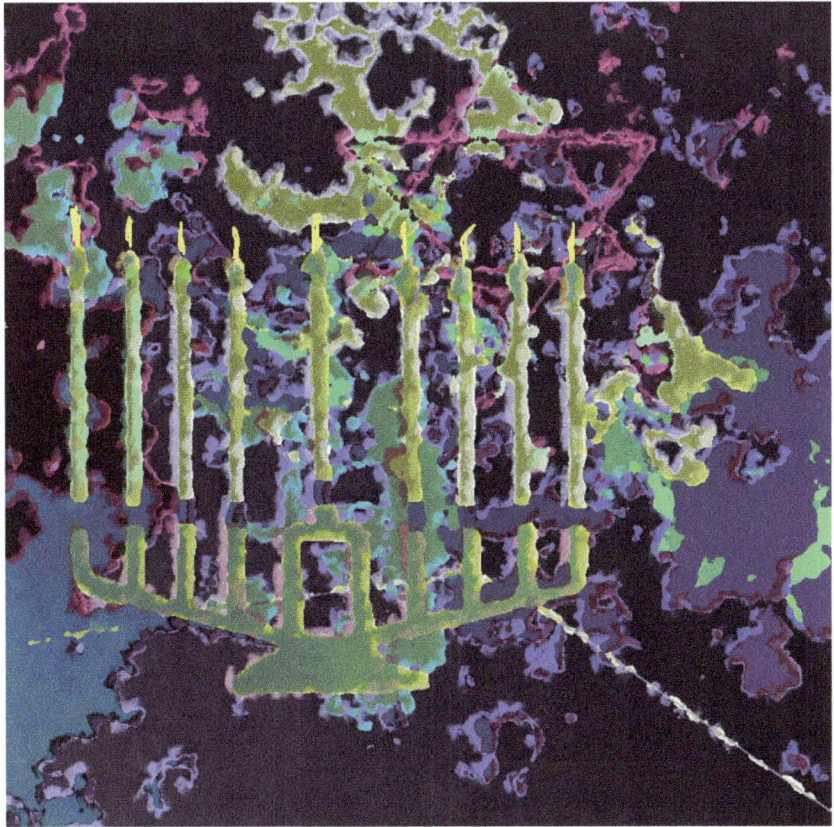

Menorah and the Star of David

Union

I've walked slowly through the spirit world, lately:
Jarring replications of Michelangelo's *Pieta* and *Moses*,
Donatello's *David*, and Singleton's *Via Dolorosa*.
At surprising moments, something like distilled vapor
passed through my body, stirring a chill, then a following
warmth and attending comfort. Airy aromas rose from
aged oak barrels falling eventually into the goblet
of my body. Spirits of this world and the other world
in union.

Ekphrastic Poem

It's almost as though these four have been
incarcerated, hastily. No standardized uniforms.
In face, two are naked, showering in front of the
others calmly, paying attention only to cleanliness.
Among those clothed, one has lulled himself to sleep,
his head pressing into the grey-white stone wall.
What comfort can there be with that pillow? He
could care less. Sleeping in filthy clothes? Why not
. . . when you've been running for days? From what?
It's anybody's guess. Has he stolen, perhaps maimed,
even taken someone's life?

I had no sooner wondered than the one clothed
in a priestly looking black and white garb wheeled
about from his directional running, up the long
staircase toward a door that would surely be bolted,
spoke loudly and angrily down to me: "Just what
business is this of yours?" I was stunned!
I sad nothing at all. I was only thinking, not speaking.
I was merely looking at and making guesses of the four
of them in this painting. "How can you, a character
painted by Jared French, be talking to me?"

"Because I am the Priest of Art Criticism and
must run up and down this long, concrete
stairway night and day forever or until someone
finds beauty in the painter's painting and buys it."

"You may have to wait for a very long time.
This is not a beautiful painting. It is filled with
pain and apparent suffering."

"But, you and all others who look to art, music, drama
must come to understand that both pain, even suffering
can be glorious in a creator's hands. God has shown you so."

The Door

I stare at the door,
crystal knob the only
light in the room. "Don't
open the door," I've been told.
One never knows what is behind
a door painted darkly obsidiean.
Coal-like, with a single gleaming eye.

A young mother told me once, "After
I send my children off to school, I walk
into the bedroom closet, shut the door
behind me and sit . . . still, on the floor
the whole of the day until I hear my children's
voices save me by their laughter on returning."

Saved by young joy, by those who love the light.
"Don't open the door," I've been told. "Don't
reach for that eye staring back at you."
One never knows what is behind such doors.
Deep fear, perhaps. A person starved for the touch
of children's hands, laughter, life. One bent
down, hiding among shoes with no feet—
One who loves life but cannot live it.

Open the Door

The Fall

Falling,
I stumbled, tumbled, hurtled
(Methuselah's time). With each roll,
cumulus clouds, from my back
danced in white: Quiet ballroom
sky while the swishing of Levi pant legs
unexpectedly blasted my ears.

Ten feet down. I thought of my childhood,
crashing against coffee table edges, crying
for help, but now I would make no sound,
not a soul near enough to hear or care, and
at age 77 too proud make a sound.

Blind Teiresias

Sleep: A Dramatic Dialogue

Why is sleep so difficult?

Each night has its own answer.

You mean every night is different?

Of course. Do you sleep with such weight about you that you don't know the rumblings of a storm, don't hear the crying of a child in the night?

A child! You don't hear a child, surely. Crying? Where?

The third house north of us.

Oh, please. That's not even possible.

I hear the whispers of his prayer as he bends his seven-year-old body at his bed.

And, he prays for what?

It's not a simple prayer, not as most seven-year-olds might pray. But, that's all I can say. I don't wish to betray his secrets.

You're being foolish now.

No, I'm being judicious.

And, this is what keeps you awake each night, eavesdropping on conversations between God and a seven-year-old boy.

No, I never hear God. He doesn't speak. And, besides, I told you each night has its own answer.

* * *

So, the prayer and God's silence was last night? And, what of the night before that? You slept very little that night, either.

Yes. The night before last was Mr. Behm's coughing. Fourteen minutes after 3, mid-morning. The cough was so wrenching I woke with a start, and as it continued, my bed clothes grew damp, my forehead warm. My legs began to crawl beneath the covers, and I finally got up and walked about the house in the dark. I'm worried about him.

And, did walking around the house help either you or him?

That's not fair. I just can't settle down long enough to sleep.

You're getting bags under your eyes. What's God gonna do about that?

Nothing, I would guess.

* * *

Okay. Three nights ago you didn't even crease the pillow.

I know.

You have any idea what . . .

Of course, I know. I don't forget these things. They're all important.
I *can't* let go of them. I'm not sure why, but I can't. It's like they carve
deep shapes somewhere in my brain.

You're not going to have anything in that cavity up there if you don't . . .

I know! I know! Don't you think I know? But, I can't let them out. It's like there's something I need to know, and I can only know by what the night . . . some night . . . will tell me. I'm memorizing every sound I hear, every glimmer of light I see, everything I smell, everything I taste after the sun sets, too . . . and our last touch before you slip into bed. All of those, and more, I know . . . when the night's pitch black.

And so, three nights ago was all of that . . . and something else, something new?
Well, the night before that . . . was that Friday night? I'm not sure . . .

Isn't it a bit ironic that you remember that child you said you heard . . . Mr. Behm . . . and all those other sensate things so clearly, but you can't count back four nights ago to Wednesday? It was Wednesday!

I don't know. Maybe I'm losing it.

Losing what?

Just losing it . . . everything.

Well, if you had said sleep, I couldn't have constructed anything that might even begin to sound like an argument that could deal with that. That's really what we've been talking about, isn't it? Losing sleep? That's what you're losing.

* * *

Okay! Got it! Do you want to hear about Wednesday night or not?

Only if it's more interesting that what I've heard so far.

Thanks for your concern.

Well . . . make it more interesting. Pull a stripper in.

Sorry. No stripper. It was a very old woman who fell.

Four houses north, I'm sure.

No, it was north, but it was the north end of town.

Oh, come on. And, you heard her.

No, I felt the pain in her back, and it radiated up my spine fiercely, all the way to the neck. She was so helpless, unable to move even so much as to push her cane away from beneath her.

And?

I don't know. She may be lying there still. I saw no one to help her. And, I could only sit in my darkened study. I closed my eyes, but not for sleep . . . for escape. I'm ashamed of that.

You're some kind of case. You know that?

I suppose. That is, if I know what you mean. I suppose there are few who have the problems with sleep I have.

You bet your damn dollar! It's about to drive me up a wall.
Well, obviously I'm getting along with it so very, very well.

Now, listen to that. That's the other thing.

There's another? More?

Yes! You make light of everything. Not a serious bone in that white sleepless body of yours.

You, obviously, haven't heard <u>anything</u> I've said. And, my rejoinder from atop my empty head is . . . perhaps you make darkness of everything, or at the least, too many dangerous darknesses, by paying so little attention to the world around you.

* * *

Well, let's see what s-c-a-r-y darkness I can find in my little man's "Sleepless in Seattle" last Friday night.

I've never been to Seattle.

That shouldn't bother you any. I'm sure you can hear those ships coming into the harbor and hear all that alphabet-soup chatter down in Chinatown.

Well, I don't like your reference, but I have to say, I've never tried.

Okay, forget it: What kept you awake Friday?

You'll just laugh.

No, I won't. I've gotten over the laughing. Try me.

You've not made this easy for me, perhaps especially this. I think it's important that this happens on the evening of the Shabbat.

Where did that come from? You're not Jewish! In our twenty years of marriage, I've never heard you use that word. Can you even spell it?

I had to look it up . . . I needed to know, just be sure.

Sure of what, just the spelling?

Well, that but something else, too. Something I heard growing up.

In Texas?

No, you know better than that. I was born in Texas, but I grew up in California. This came from some of my buddies out there who were devout Jews.

What exactly came from this theologically reliable source, pray tell? Oh, you see? I've got some humor in me, too: "pray" tell?

Yeah. Got it. I'm not asleep, you know.

Touché.

This one is more specific, graphic, and, yet, I was riveted even when I wanted to look away.

Now *this* sounds more interesting. What town this time?

Afghanistan. No town. Just desert. Hard to see anything, the dust inflicted pain.

You mean you felt it?

My face felt pocked, eyes, when I could open them, bled.

Now surely . . .

Please, hear me out. This is important . . . Through slits in my eyes, I saw something move. I sharpened my focus to see that it was a young American medic, bent over another soldier lying inert beneath him. The medic had a Cross of David hanging around his neck. I heard him whisper to the poor guy, "Hold on. It'll be okay." He'd just gotten the word "okay" out of his mouth when an explosion blasted my ears and lifted those two young bodies high into the air. Don't you see? . . . I had not heard a single sound until I heard that whisper. Then, all hell turned them and me inside out! It shattered the air, then fell completely silent when those two bodies finally hit the ground. I can't forget these things. Let them make my eyes bleed, crash about my ears. Make me blind. Take my hearing. I don't hear what I need to hear, after all. I wait, I expect . . . night after night a voice . . . a voice to tell me why, oh, why.

* * *

The problem isn't sleep, is it?
Well, yes. Of course it is.

No, it's the voice. The voice you never hear.

I don't understand what you're saying.

That little crying guy, Mr. Behm, the lady perhaps still lying in the floor, those young, helpless warriors . . . they all need help. Damn it all! The world needs help. But, there's no voice that says, "I'm here. I'll take care of it." Or a voice that says, "I won't ever let this happen again." You've listened for

God's voice every night this week, and because all you have heard is silence . . . well, you're not even sure, any longer that there is a God. Go ahead. Cry your bleeding eyes out. Then, go to sleep. You have your answer. There is no voice. But, maybe . . . just maybe, there's something else.

Tree Shells Against the Sky

A Young Boy's Flight

Exacto knife in right hand,
balsawood in my left—
Judy Garland's voice lilting
through a dark night from
the next street, and I carve
the wings of the P-38 that will fly,
in time, to an incredulous height.

I must choose the softest of sandpapers,
brush my diminutive wings, make them
smooth—light, and have them rise
to "Somewhere Over the Rainbow,"
to meet Judy there.

Live Wires

Barcarolle

The prow of the gondola noses
into the narrow grotto opening.
Refracted blues of water and sky
splash dazzling sunlight
to the cave's stone ceiling.
Cerulean shades.

An oarsman stands tall
at the stern of the craft,
guides us from breathtaking light
into deepening darknesses.
His throaty, songful voice resounds
through our now black cavernous world.

Elegant sounds then aggregate, extended silence.
Aware of our discomfort, he eases us toward
the luminous opening we first entered.
Light. Darkness. Light again. Melody. Silence.
Being. Who is this oarsman?

I Am Well

I am well, really.
I smiled when she left.
I, Don Quixote, lay my sword down.
Sancho looked at me quizzically.
But I am well. Sancho knows that nothing has power over me.
Sword now in sheath, protected from loss.
Do know this. I am well. Very well.

     * * *

Forgive me for these lies.

Job's Song

I remember a certain
stillness once
but now the winds whirl,
touching my bones
through the tattered cloak
I wear like torn flesh.
Ashes blind me in their swirl,
dust grinds its way
into the redness flowering
in my sores, and I sing.

I sing a song of questions,
I sing a song of love.
I rage once more for answers,
only winds come from above.
Must I forever wonder
while these worms yet crawl my skin?
Must restlessness still taunt me,
I, upright of men?

For one fraction of eternity
I heard a voice antiphonal.
Surely, as anything can be sure,
the voice was His.
Winds are my sole melodies now,
encircling me, driving me to
the center of aloneness, and I sing.

I sing a song of quiet,
I sing a song of love.
I beg once more for answers,
still winds come from above.
Must I forever wonder
while these worms yet crawl my skin?
Must restlessness still taunt me,
I, upright of men?

The winds blow through empty
spaces in the pages of my song.
Little but the wind is not dying.
Flesh and song alike crawl

with decay and my throat grows
dry. I can sing no longer, of that
I am sure . . . yet I sing.

I sing a song of parched throat,
I sing a song of love.
I will ask no more for answers,
only cease the winds above.
I know that I must wonder,
I know I cannot know.
I know beyond all questions,
I know, my God, I know!

I know that I am weary.
I doubt I can longer sing.
I know my voice will leave me
like a thrush on injured wing.
Jaweh, of creation,
in the time that yet remains,
create in me fresh music.
Make me breathe new life again.
Once I sang with boldness,
but, oh, my songs are weak.
Dear God, I can't remember
when all seemed so damned and bleak.

   * * *

Crying the day,
cursing the night toward forever,
his voice seemed the voice of confusion
matching winds of no direction.
Only time and necessity would form his shouts
into whispers and make of them an imperceptible
rustling of leaves, and song.

   * * *

I sing a song of no words,
I sing news songs of love.
I now see with certain stillness,
I have nothing to be proved.
I give you, God, my quiet,
You give me peace in its stead.

We give ourselves to the other,
there is nothing to be said.

My song is too long in singing,
but quiet seems often so.
Dear, God, of all creation,
help me in my silence grow.
Make me know timeless wonder,
give me awe at what You've done.
And I will give you Job
with the setting of each quiet sun.

Don't Run

Is there a place devoid of fragility?
Is all broken, already the child's new toy,
the once smoothly-paved street, now
(or forever) pot-holed by the latest storm,
or the seeming well-oiled heart in almost
anyone's body?

Is there nothing we can turn to and say,
"Aah, there! That's sturdy. It'll stand the
test of long-grinding time." And, the slightest
crack begins, just a little porcelain chip that
gives way to some weakness within and
gravity without, and then gone.

We are all broken. I don't know why or when
it invades us, this brokenness, but it possesses
a relentlessness. No need to run, no matter
how swift you are. It will ease its way into you
or crash upon you like some falling timber.
It will make a noise whether you are in a
forest or not, whether with someone of alone.
    Well, perhaps never really alone.

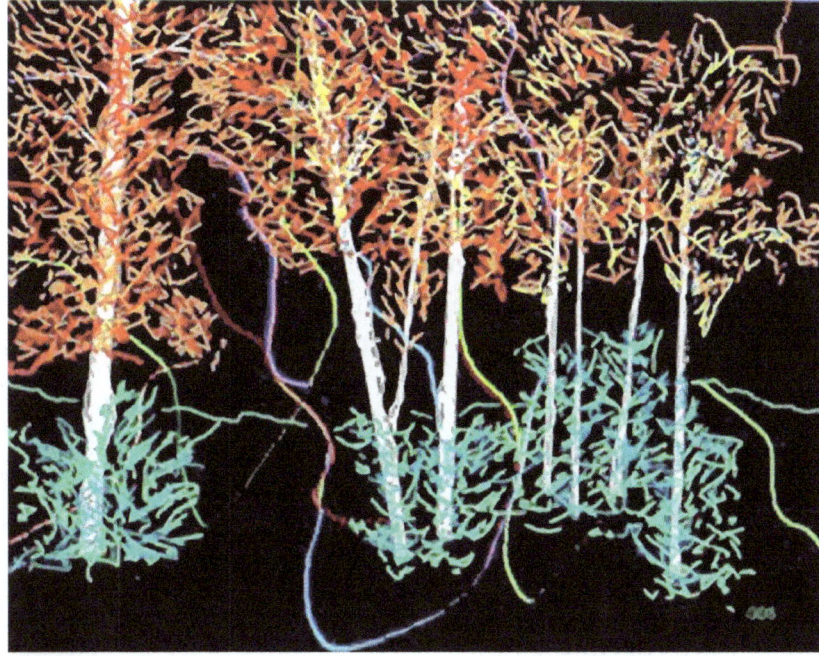

Birches

Andy's Apologia

I.
Andy's attempt at words moves through spittle, imperceptible—moist.
A towering spire over diminished mother and father, his motions rag-doll
him from one side of the room to the other, nervously: gangly giraffe lolling
among other aimless beasts of the world. He is forty, going on seven,

perhaps less. No one knows for sure. It's known only that on most days
he inhabits his gawky form with grace. No one confuses
this day, however, with just any day. Andy will be baptized.
He will reel under the weight of a significance he'll not understand.

Raw inelegance. No grace.
On the savanna, such a lonely living thing would, in confusion,
be prey to the lion. But here, Andy will be surrounded
by well-intentioned ones who'll claw at his innocent, empty head,
use sharpened theologies to pull his carcass into water, and drown him
with love.

II.
He is down, deep down in water where blue cotton candy floats
beneath eyelids and cold waves blouse loose white cloth
about arms and legs and chest.
Filaments of hair rise . . . fall . . . twist in frightened lives of their own.

And Andy is unknowing, a timorous animal held under water
by officious, ecclesiastical hands though he can only guess why.
His body pleads for release, reaches for air, but is pulled lower and lower
until he knows the release must be his: "Give in, give way! Let it gush

up through nostrils—down through throat, wash away my loneliness,
take me where I can understand something . . . anything at all."

III.
His form rises to the surface, pure white flotsam.
He steps from the pool, feels the cloth clasp about his body,

constricting blood flow to every part of him.
The minister intones resonant words of consolation:

"You are saved, saved. Dear Andy, you are saved,"
and Andy looks longingly back, into deep . . . deep candy-blue water.

Footloose

Discomfort

Ordinarily, (is anything ever ordinary?)
I look at a branch as I walk even a short
distance, and hasten my cane-laden
pace more hurriedly.

Now what new sign in nature compels my
legs and hips to move more rapidly than
my neuropathy-labored feet? Ahh, there!
A place to rest. But, as I begin my turn
of gesture, I see for the first time, bar-like slats
on both the seat and the back of benches
in a row. My full body weight recoils, and I've
jerked away from them so recklessly, I near a fall.

I see angry, despairing men and women imprisoned
over our countryside: Blacks, Hispanics, the occasional
Anglo (mostly Blacks though). Sharply or sullenly angry
—through epithets thrown at me, through eyes cast
down to filthy floors, or heads jutted to the cell ceilings,
repeating, "Why? Dammit, why?"

And, I know, too, that the shouts I hear, the rabid faces
I see say, "You are free to walk away from this little
bench in front of you for the discomfort you will feel,
      but only for only a moment or so."

The Birth of Ishmael

> *"The angel of the Lord also said to her: 'You are now with child and you will have a son. You shall name him Ismael, for the Lord has heard of your misery. He will be a wild donkey of a man; his hand will be against everyone and everyone's hand against him, and he will live in hostility toward all his brothers.'"* Genesis 16:11-12

Legs splayed wide
From Kadesh to Bered,
Hagar bore Ishmael.
The feathery one called him
a donkey, an ass of a man.
He flailed as an unborn child, kicked
like a four-legged beast, then spilled
from inside the handmaiden's womb
onto blistering desert sands at the edge
of Shur—plastique explosives strapped

    to his soft, small underbelly.

Circumcision (*brit milah*)

"Cut it away from bone.
It'll never be missed," You say,

As if you could know.
"Let it fall onto the cutting table
like a useless piece of meat
unfit for sacrifice."

This is how you treat old men,
my thirteen-year-old son, and each
eight-day-old male child?
Fit only to have private parts
slashed away? Do we need another
enemy, Jaweh? More than Egypt,
Elam, Ellasar.

                      * * *

The knife kissed soft foreskin while the bone
under flesh stiffened as for an act of love.
A crimson opulence streamed over Caanan—
Abram, now Abraham; Sarai, now Sarah and progeny:
Countless Jews tramping toward Jerusalem,
Numberless Ishmaelites, now Arabs, swaggering
to Mecca—all slinging M-14s over shoulders, moving mutilated
toward an indistinct future.

Number Thirteen

Called number 13 for as long as I can remember, its circularity represents synonymically almost everything that finds its way into an eight-inch form sitting languidly by my desk. Its mouth, always yawing widely takes whatever is thrown its way. And, it's usually a sharp, angry, or disappointed toss that propels the "whatever": lyric poems, sonnets, pantoums that get started and die, at the bottom of the can . . . ink barely dry but quickly comparable to a dead rabbit fried on the floor of the Mohave Desert.

How many rabbits have I slain? "Don't throw anything away," I tell my student writers and myself. But, most of those rabbits die, if not by what seems like desert heat, then by a strangling from the smell of rotting bad vending machine aroma or by smothering from papers, and other heavy useless office equipment. What might happen if I were to reach down into that abyss and
drag away a castaway?

Let's see, should I not throw away anything at all? Okay, I did it, went against everything I've taught for fifty or more years, and here it is:

> I was sitting in my porch chair, thinking about nothing
> . . .

I don't even have a porch with a chair on it, but I'm always thinking about something. Not that day when I shot that piece of paper into the trash can . . . two points, but nothing I'd ever want anyone to see as a piece of my work. This time, the paper landed on something sticky, looking like glue mixed with some cookie crumbs. Right where it belongs. Not about to reach in for that again. Just need to be sure none of my students drops by.

Need to throw everything out, now, or I might hear, "Nice guy, but a liar."

Were I to Write a Letter

I.
How might I address it? What might the cost be?
Forget the cost! But, can I address it General Mail
and expect him to get it? No street address, no
city or state . . . or country, for that matter. Nothing.
Nothing but a name, and the memory of my holding
him in my arms as he drew his last breath.

A father, though not mine. He seemed so even
though I had a father once. I have no address for
him, either. Perhaps they have become close to
one another. I'd like that. He would, too. Both
such uncommon men: compassionate, almost to a fault,
creative in differing ways, respected in every way.

I had no opportunity to talk with Pop in his dying
days. I only knew what he thought about living
and dying by the peaceful way he appeared to leave
this earth. But how can I talk to him now and know
everything I need to know, want to know, must know?
How? Perhaps the Postal Office can help. Two letters.

II.
Gordon (my philosophy professor, my mentor, my Provost)
and I (his student, his protégé, his Dean . . . at his request),
in extended conversations over months. He had asked me
to sit with him, having learned of his terminal cancer, to
both listen and talk with him about living and dying. I had
wanted to say, "I can't. You're too close to me," and said,

"Yes, of course. You are so close to me." We did, wonderfully,
until his hand grew limp in mine. Never, in all my studies
of almost all books available to me have I come to know so
much and now . . . don't ask me why now, I don't know . . . but
I must write to him and to my biological father. I can only write
letters, but I must write letters. Someone, please, tell me,

"Where can I send them?"

Buddhist Prophet in Standing Meditation

Benny and the Gang

Sitting in a comfortable chair, house empty. I've been walking through The Benny Goodman Story on TV, enjoying every Jewish moment of the film (story for another poem). Never so drawn in. Then, the conclusion: Carnegie Hall and *Sing, Sing, Sing*, with Benny on Clarinet, of course, Harry James on Trumpet, Gene Krupa on drums, and Teddy Wilson on piano. Quintet with full band. I began crying uncontrollably.

A few days later, I finished delicious wanderings through Chaim Potok's *The Gift* and burst into resplendent tears. A year or so earlier, aboard a cruise to Egypt, I sat on the deck with a sea breeze blowing the pages of Toni Morrison's latest work, *Jazz*, finding the rhythm of her lines to be their own jazz riffs, and at its close, I began to cry. Each of these emotional moments reached a location somewhere in my brain that celebrated excellence.

Perhaps more crying would help all of us to meet our every-day more dizzying world.

Trio II

Eschatology

They crowd the seeded feeder
in turn: Cassin's Finches, Cardinals,
Song and Harris' Sparrows, occasional
Black-throated Grays, and Blue Jays.

A congress of daily dying,
living out three-year life spans
with wing-fluttering frenzy.

Do they, as they gather for perhaps
a last meal, talk of death?
What must they say? "I have only days
to live. What will become of my little ones?
Life seems so short."
Do they talk of trees and skies beyond these,
of shapes and colors never seen? Metaoaks?
Metaskies?

As thousands die each day,
where do their small bodies go?
Are they whisked away from treetops at dawn,
a multi-colored rapture that gives reds and blues
to the early morning sky?

Are those gentle winds I hear, the fleeing
movements of wings toward another world?
Are they deep-throated songs,
final exhalations of commingled
small breaths?

Night Feeding

A Professor's Perspective, and . . .

So little time is left. What can I possibly do? The world passes away.
Will Rilke or Frankl ever be read again? Can Odysseus find his way
to Ithaka? I'm not certain I have enough time to show him, and he doesn't know the story of the
continuing journey.

* * *

Rest your mind, old man. Perhaps someone, it needn't be you,
can lend him a timeless MS of Constantine Cavity's "Ithaka"
or teach him from the splendor of that wondrous poet's words
that neither Odysseus nor Rilke nor Frankl, nor any other man
or woman should fret the passage of tomorrow, not with the sun
shining so brightly today.

Seaman's Leisure Reading

Upright Blues in the Key of F

F　　　'notha night here in Sammy Blues'
　　　　slappin' the guts, 'ccasional drink of booze
　　　　standin' here lookin' down at my shoes

B♭　　 left hand wrapped 'round her tight
　　　　right hand pickin' a sullen fight
　　　　with a new piano player, black on white

C⁷　　 i'm winnin' *this* fracas, hands down
　　　　he's some kinda lazy, crazy clown
　　　　but he plays those keys real good, uptown

F　　　guitar player's been 'round long, long time
　　　　been in and out, on every crime
　　　　but listen to him now, he's 'bout to climb

B♭　　 those strings, I mean, from bottom to top
　　　　they ain't nobody I'd wanta swap
　　　　probably get some silk-pant fop

C⁷　　 lady joe is singin' it sweet
　　　　with a real nice, soft, syncopated beat
　　　　she ain't nothin' if she ain't discrete

F　　　with her low gravelly voice, top notch goods
　　　　what we do, right here, together's beatitude
　　　　but now it's over. . .now, well-earned solitude
　　　　what we do, right here, together's beatitude
　　　　but now it's over . . . now, well-earned solitude

Standup Bass Rambler Rattlers

Scott Joplin Reminisces

1915. He sits, shoulders rounded, still caressin' the keys at his fingers.
It's *Reflection Rag* in a posh concert hall, not knowin' he will die, 1917.
He drifts and dreams, aching bones, black face, dark eyes still smilin'.

He grins when he plays, and mustard gas fills the grand room, colorin'
the ivories yellow as he glides. One year into a war that will end all wars.
All wars, forever more. He laughs, with syncopation, beneath his breath.

1909. In Chicago, a shotgun house, 1 a.m. He plays *Solitude*, a haunting
rag, sittin' in his room alone, sippin' whiskey from a glass on the piano.
He remembers the day Honus Wagner hit an in-the-park home run

'gainst the Cubs. The NAACP was just created, but he's still alone. He can't
know the crash of '29 will quiet the jangles of Bang 'Em Bar. No skirts
lifted. Only quiet leaps from vaulting buildings or nights with no food.

1907. It's a *Sunflower Slow Day*, and he rags the keys in Sedalia, MO.
Back home again where it nearly all began: piano serenades for the poor
and the rich, from the share-croppin' farmer to black tie and tails.

Makes no difference. Music's for all, whether you're eatin' just potatoes
or sippin' champagne. Good to be home, he thinks, as he sees the trees
turnin' red while he plays *Maple Leaf Rag* and thinks to 1899.

Applause halts his reverie at the end of *Reflection Rag*. He bends in a mature,
still graceful bow, hears the clapping of hands from Texarkana, Sedalia, Chicago,
New York. Remembers, most of all, the trees from each place, swayin' like music.

The birches, the maples, and most the Cyprus growing out of Caddo Lake near
his place of birth, stately moss hanging from top branches, touching water.
He'll not play ragtime much longer.

Slow Touch on the Keys

Gravity (I)

I have carried gravitas in my person.
Heavy luggage pulling me down into
stentorian outcries at scars inflicted
on the world's face.

I lie here now, unable to move
arms or legs. Unable to speak. Tangles
of wires, apparatuses playing with torpid
body. Pressure cuff on the right arm tightening
to ask if blood has found its way (without benefit
of GPS) through the mitral valve to unknown
destinations. It loosens its grasp. A breathy sigh
suggests uncertainty.

My mind, mistakenly interred in a dying
body, wanders through the Oxford English
Dictionary, discovering the Old French *gravite*,
then falls into a six-feet hole dug deep in the earth's
face. And I cry out, again, for wounds trenched
blithely in bruised soil.

Gravity (II)

From somewhere above, great hands
press down. The sky weighs heavily
with blue atoms pushing the back of my head
deep into this damnable white pillow.

Unable to turn my head right or left,
I stare, understanding that if my legs
can't move, my arms can't move, then
why would my head deign to believe

it is somehow special. If described
with accuracy, the brain's a small casing housing
pulpy lobes of flesh swimming in cerebrospinal
fluid. I wonder if . . .

Ahh! It still *wonders* while hearing Peggy Lee's
"Is That All There Is?" My neurologist wondered,
too. "Is this all there is?" But, I heard her
singing! I'm in here someplace.

Look at my face. I entered this hospital five
months ago. Face like a winding road twisting,
curving around my wide-open Taos Gorge-like mouth,
picket-fenced

by discoloring teeth. Look at me now.
My face, the face of a child, smooth,
white hair bedraggled for lack of attention
(since I can't move my hands), but look, *my face*.

I'm the Gerber baby who just heard a torch
song. Peggy Lee. I may be no Einstein,
but I'm here. Look at me. Look at me.
And, my neurologist says, "That face?" Ahh,
just gravity.

Exhalations

I'll never understand the flash of one's
last breath . . .
ephemeral, an almost negligible slip of air exiting the body,
then gone.
The breath of some, of course, must, after years and years of living—even dying,
fly away.
That I comprehend, at some trivial level akin to understanding
nursery rhymes.

> "Now I lay me down to sleep, I pray the Lord my soul
> to keep . . ."

Or perhaps I only think I know. A hand grasps a fly swatter. I do not
grasp dying.
The young, lungs filled with fragrances from seedtime flowers—why must
they die?
Shouldn't diaphragms in callow chests move in then out, in then out,
over and over, again and again.

* * *

Enough dancing around flying exhalations! It's war and its squalid breath-
snatching, life-filching bombast I hate, its need to strike down the innocent,
generation after generation—breathing in and out, in and out, over and over . . .

Egret in Flight

Masks

Slime your way surreptitiously,
slide like syrup to down-stage center.
The mask you wear in this American
tragedy is the liar's, needing two faces
one pointing forward, the other behind
your back, and this moment's victim.

Yeah, pull that blade from your scabbard.
Plunge it deep in the gut. Stand tall
in traitorous *kathurni*, making you look
larger than life, you smaller-than-life
rapscallion. The scene's turned bloody
with each jab from your left hand.

No one to clean the mess, this slip and
slide, but you, the liar who started it all.
You're not about to clean anything. You
only walk away, that's your real life. No
stage hands in this drama, just you and
your counterpoint who wears no mask
at all.

Theatre Masks

Coda

How precisely do we end this piece?
Is there a soul who can tell us how?
Gone through hundreds of hypotheses.

Clashing cymbals? Grace notes to appease?
Piano Arpeggio, somehow?
How precisely do we end this piece?

What of musical soliloquies?
Played from the heart, with attending bow.
Gone through hundreds of hypotheses.

I have considered antitheses,
None has ever worked, but anyhow . . .
How precisely do we end this piece?

Life is but closed parentheses,
Some say, but I simply can't allow.
Gone through hundreds of hypotheses.

God, give me something that can appease,
Make it a Memphis blues riff. Ahh, wow!
How precisely do we end this piece?

Gone through hundreds of hypotheses.

Crosby Stills and Nash

I Have Travelled

    —for Mary

I have travelled the land, the skies:
Tuscany, Bavaria, Estonia, Cloud Nine,
even touched Cloud 13 with the tip
of one finger, have caught the right
foot of St. Paul on his journey to
7th Heaven.

It wasn't until I saw you smile that . . .
Well . . . I saw you smile, and travelled
farther than ever before.

The smile, your smile, was the width
of the Danube, no . . . no, the widest
reach of the Mississippi. It was as if
I found myself in a large, wheel-turning
Delta craft, languidly floating your smile.
I could not see the shore of either side.

I have now forgotten Tuscany, other lands,
and all numbered heavens. I have your smile
and have made it mine.

Woman's Face Study

Daughters, Do Not Weep for Me

"All of you," Jesus said, "and you daughters of the land,
you have walked far to be with me, in my sorrow.
I have seen your tears. And, I am tired," he says, "as are you,
but do not weep for me. Because you have heard my word,
and do not truly hear and have not understood what awaits
you. Because you do not know what awaits me, it is I who
weeps for you."

Murmurings grow among the crowd surrounding Jesus.
Questioning, even angry words ripple from their mouths.
One speaks boldly: "Here are His riddles again." Jesus
stretches His arms outward as if begging to join the hands
of his puzzled followers with Jaweh's. "No dear ones,
here is your riddle." He lifts his head skyward, closes his eyes
tightly, and says,

"Myrrh, a gift for me at my birth, is taken from the Commiphora
tree. Aromatic, bitter-to-the-taste resin flows from each branch
where spikes have been driven, and as it falls to the ground,
hardening into droplets of white tears, a sweet-smelling aroma
fills the whole of the valley where trees grow." "Master," a woman
says, "I am sorry. I do not understand."

On hearing the soft voice of the woman, Jesus opens his eyes and says,
"I have walked sands, hot to the touch of my feet in the direction of
Golgotha, carrying in my body a rich, red gift to be spilled freely
over the earth. When spikes tear through flesh, tears will fall. And,
in all the valleys of all the trees, there will be a sweet, sweet smell."

Crux

A Reading

She was an apparition
as she materialized before
her audience wearing literary
dignity like a cloak wrapped blackly
about a thin frame. She read, light
frothy poems at first, evoking mandatory
titters from a gathering of knowing listeners
dressed in polite gray. Then she set them aside,
audience and poems alike, like single sheets
of thin, frivolous paper, and reached deep
down where vital organs
live.

Miniature narratives she called
them, exercises, warm-ups for the big stuff,
stuff that stumbles into anthologies to be
read by freshmen frocked in pink
in Biloxi, Mississippi.

She read with a certain casualness
at first, adjusting occasionally, dark stringy
hair falling over her equally dark-rimmed
glasses. Something about a woman sitting
in an empty house listening for the closing
of a door, I think. I didn't really hear
the words. But I tasted them. Acrid
to the tongue, frightened, desolate.
And as they wore on, with a certain tragic
theatricality, I thought she grew noticeably
uncertain of words her own pale lips formed,
as if too bitter for the mouth, too painful
for her ears, too lonely to be so. Momentarily,
she stopped, turned her back on an audience
long forgotten, just remembered,
and gathered what composure could
be gathered into the small white school-teacher
blouse I now noticed she was wearing.

Turning back again, eyes yet moist, showing
a soft blue embarrassment, she suggested someone
else might need to finish her little story, but

the silence pushed her on to the very last word, when she vanished from her listeners only to be seen two years later in a new anthology, under short fiction.

White Hat

Black and White Rag

> "Do not play this piece fast. It is
> never right to play Ragtime fast."
> –Scott Joplin

Let it play lentando
in Chicago's searing heat.
Treat it andantino
to Miami's brooding beat.
Syncopate the cadence,
counter every black with white.
Make them taste soulful rhythm
in my Ragtime dirge tonight.

I wrote it jeremiad
with white keys laid on black,
so let it play itself sad
the sole song in town, Jack.
It's one man on the treble
and one man on the bass,
as each plays his cleft to the color of his face.

Play appassionato,
it's wrong to play it fast.
Yea, slip it in the marrow,
Slow . . . gentle to the last.
A black man's soul brought down hard
in the face of a white man's spite,
that's my syncopated score
to be settled by tonight.

Blow!

Fugue

> —from the French: a flight and/or amnesiac state of mind.
> Also a musical form or composition

A minor key strikes at my ears
Only a few steps from the blonde cashier,
And I brazenly become a sonneteer

Filled with words, rhythms, and pageant.
Sounding somewhat, a bit, like the Earl of Kent
Loaded up with a single-malt scotch, opulent

With locution and quite full of myself.
I'm astonishingly loud: the shout of a Guelph
'Gainst the Ghibellines. I'm standing by a shelf

Of crackers and canned sardines. I turn around,
Feeling I've suddenly become strangely unwound
By something beyond my power. I see horehound

Wrapped in a shimmering blue, good for the cough.
I reach for it to the cadence of Rachmaninoff,
Piano Concerto # 3, Opus 30. I then take off

In the direction of Aisle #3 in hopes of seeing . . .
I don't know what . . . I'm running, running, running
Past aisles 4 and 5 and, help me God! I'm singing

Lyrics I've never heard before.
It's almost as though I held a score
In my hands, racing throughout the store

Looking for the Maestro who penned the Rach 3.
I hold the perfect lyrics for him to see.
That's what I, at the least, thought: a symphony

By Rachmaninoff and Benjamin Britten
It has always been my ultimate aim
To acquire a well-earned, lavishing fame

With my words coupled to music I idolize.
Someone's chasing me, so I must improvise.

I pick from a shelf Windex and atomize

The one who's pursued me from among the breads.
I'm racing mindlessly in my head,
Jumping boxes, stacks of foods, then shed

My shoes as quickly as I can.
When I do, I knock down crates and crates of bran.
They're all over the floor . . . and . . . and,

I have no idea where I am.
The first thing to mind is Rotterdam.
It's all like some devilish cryptogram.

Rachmaninoff was born in Novgorod!
My head is aching, about to explode
When the 2nd Movement begins . . . *Intermezzo: Adagio,*

And my heart begins to slow its pace.
Such music in my soul, such remarkable grace:
The grand piano hovers just above the string bass,

I stop by the spinach and collard greens,
Can think of nothing but cornbread—red beans
And my grandmother's large white tureen

Of pot liquor made from dark green juice.
Rach's 2nd Movement turns into blues,
And I hear Lead Belly's three chords diffuse

My need to run and run and run and run
So, I'm back from where I first had begun.
And they tie me, roll me just past the cinnamon.

I am done. I am done. I am done. I am done.

Piano Fortissimo

'Zounds!

The vampires at my door again.
If I deny them entrance, it'll be only
moments before they will have torn
the usually welcoming entrance from
recalcitrant hinges. And so . . .

I open the door, greet them with
feigned smile, then lie compliantly
on the couch (usual place) and wait.
Franco, the older of the two (his dark,
drawn flesh and tired, deepened voice)
speaks of his plans. "I'm weary
of the neck. Let's do the arms."

Zach asks, "May I have the left?
It appears plump with rushing *blut*.
Franco replies acridly, "No! *That*
will be mine. Move away!"
Now, each in his established place,
oblivious to the pain I'm about to have
for the third time this day, begins with
probes.

"Aagghh." My vocabulary truncated.
A sucking sound climbs my spine
and heightens even as they quietly close
the door. From out of clean, white
nurses' uniforms, they say in union
as they leave, "Sorry. Sorry."

Nibblings

He said, "I can't talk with anyone else
like this. Gut stuff. All other conversation's
sham, just cocktail party nibblings. Nod
a head here, laugh there, funny or not.
Smile a lot. Scripted by some dull Disney
writer."

I didn't know if I should smile (a lot) or not,
but something rippled up my face, I'm sure.
I thought I understood . . . and said, "It's raw
because we've learned how to say I don't know,
and that's okay. In a world that believes
it must and does know, there's nothing left
of interest. No mystery. No pursuit, so it drinks
its whiskey sour, nods its head, laughs here
and there, and rolls Walt's films of emaciated,
stick-like, cartoon figures over and over again,
knowingly.

St. Francis and Friends

Now or Later?

Sitting in S.M.U's high-domed Dallas Hall built
109 years ago, I wonder how much of our world
can stand much longer. I start teaching in thirty
minutes.

Should I warn them that words will soon (any
moment) become ICBM's? Perhaps . . . better
not.

Think I'll wait till the class is over. Missiles to
missiles, ego pitted against ego. And, our
older-than-God Dallas Hall will stand no longer,
no matter its stoic splendor, soon to be splinters.

Think I'll just wait. After seminar is over, I can't
tell them now. When it hits the fan, we (the fan)
will all lie together on the ground . . . with stone,
plaster, and sheetrock our covers while we grow
cold.

I would guess some might be strewn along steps
scaling down to the tree-lined quad. They'll enjoy
comfort from enormous walnut stumps atop them,
branches under.

Ten minutes and they're beginning to come in.
I just can't bring myself to tell them right off.
No way to start a class. How many might drop?

And, they would miss Annie Dillard's *An American
Childhood*, also how to write their own life stories
. . . better to tell them now. Let them spend the next
thirty minutes or so.

Can you image their conclusions?

SMU's Dallas Hall

Spoken Words Heal

I've watched them, carefully,
never knowing what any of them
might say. It's a memoir course.
They're talking about things deep
down where they live.

Perhaps, the moment they heard
from Mom or Dad, "We're not able
to live together any longer" or "We
haven't loved each other for a long
time."

And, then, from words far more
brutalizing, pain of strident memory
(memory is, after all, a whore),
takes on the shape-shifted form of
tears flooding the eyes, turned downward.

But, they mystically create a balm
for the cleanly-washed face. And, all
this time, I have, unnoticed, cried,
watching, listening to words, deeply
buried, rise to the surface, and heal.

An Old Writer's Interview

    —The topic: Where are you now?

That's not a very interesting question.
Not a question for a writer, or anyone.

You're not asking where I live, are you?
This virulent place is a faceless venue.

More succulence in where I've been, outside the U.S. of A.
That piques me more like Tina Fey

Playing Palin—Michael or Sarah?
Aah! Sarah. Spot on, as an arrow.

Not Sarah, of course,
But Tina Fey perforce.

And your question was . . . ?
My mind drifts away, because . . .

But, well, you never mind.
Would you be so kind

As to ask me once more?
Memory's such a whore.

I ramble on and on.
I think my synapses are entirely gone.

My interviews are deadly bores.
I meander till my interviewer snores,

Inevitably, it seems.
I often wonder what they dream,

Where they've been.
Would you like some gin?

Aah, yes. Where they've been.
I have a scotch, it's a blend,

But still quite good, I think.
Let me pour you some kind of drink.

No? You wanta get back to work.
Where did you say that was? New York?

Now, I asked you where "you are."
Would have been more intrigued had it been Ecuador.

But, then, we can't all be in tantalizing places.
Now there a writer would see interesting faces.

But, back to your question, I suppose
You likely need to bring this thing to a close.

Let's see, where have I been over my many years?
Are you sure you wouldn't have a beer?

No? Alright, then let me get started.
. . . Oh, God, I think I just farted.

My apologies to you, good man.
There are some things I just don't understand.

It's old age and all that goes with it.
I mean . . . it's almost every time that I sit

I get a bit comfortable, and who knows how it occurs,
But some rumbling sound emanates from me, or worse.

I apologize. Please know I meant no offense.
Doesn't the room smell a little like frankincense?

Back to business. I owe you some thoughts.
If any of those flitting birds can be caught.

Where am I now? No, where have I been?
I once spent three weeks in a Scottish glen.

Fiftieth wedding anniversary. It was more than grand.
My wife and I stood on a strand

By the Firth of Forth
Near a whimsical Scottish seaport.

Didn't fall dark 'till ten at night,
When the glistening seagulls quit their flight

And nestled into grass tufts near the edge of the shore.
Could a writer, with a wife of fifty years, ask anything more?

Unless it might be another fifty years
Say! I've got some Scottish beer

Called *Old Chub*. It's really an ale,
Dark . . . dark, color of dirty shale

But one of the best, the Scotsmen say.
What would they know, hey?

That word "dark" just shot me away
To Capri's Blue grotto, the edge of an Aegean Bay.

Now, *that's* about as dark as dark can be.
There were only us three, us three.

It was my wife, the gondolier, and I,
And, I can't even begin to amplify

On the wonder of the black beneath the caves.
Somewhat as I imagine graves,

But lustrous beyond compare.
The first word to mind is . . . *Claire*.

That's French for the word clear.
We were thrown back in time with our sea charioteer.

What an occasion this was. I'll never forget.
Romeo, who died young, you know, and his coquette

Rowed beneath black walls with resonating sounds.
To this very bright day I'm spellbound

By how light and dark live in such adjacency.
And whether from the tomb I shall be able to see

Those I love dearly, love the most.
Could I offer you a piece of toast?

No? Then, let's see. Where was I?
My mind, I'm sorry, is like a butterfly.

It takes flight about . . . whatever the room.
Let me come back again to the tomb.

My head puzzles nightly, alright, daily, too
About death, its implications. What else would I do

At ninety-three, soon ninety-four?
I can only tell you that I deplore

The idea of hitting some ball a hundred yards or so
Into grizzly grass some caretaker refused to mow.

Now, caretaker prods me to think of the grave again.
I buried my father's ashes, his only remains

Not a sinew of flesh was left in the urn.
When I think of him, it gives me concern

That he has no mouth with which he can speak.
When I think of it and think of it, everything's bleak.

I need a gentle voice to calm me at times.
Wanna play a game with some beer and dimes?

Can't afford quarters. I'm too broke for that.
Writers don't make much. Did I say I'm a Democrat?

We're for the guy, guys like me.
Guys who write sonnets with boring spondee.

No one makes money writing poems, it seems.
We just do it at times because we must scream

To be heard
And hope that some editor turd

Will hear us and deign to accept
What she thinks is reasonably adept,

And, so it falls into some journal that no one reads.
They'd rather hit the stock market and sate their greed.

That's why I'm a Democrat. Would you like some cheese?
Goes nice with some bourbon. I can get it with ease.

No again? Okay, I'll get to your point.
I certainly wouldn't want to disappoint

Your turd, meaning editor, of course.
I think I'm beginning to get a little bit hoarse.

Where was I now? Oh, yes, places to be.
More correctly, places I've been, places you should see.

Salisbury. Spires reaching out of sight,
Like eagles shooting skyward in dangerous flight.

Oh, yeah. Been to the hospital once or twice.
Once for a lifetime, ten times overnight.

Acid reflux, etcetera, etcetera, etcetera,
I could add to the list, plethora on plethora,

But I just noticed you look at your watch.
Oops! Sorry. Got an itch in my crotch.

What was it I just asked you?
Gotta tell you I don't have a clue.

I've got some topnotch scotch . . . topnotch scotch.
Have you ever noticed this damned blotch

On the side of my face?
What a terrible, terrible shame to deface

This great big puss of mine.

Oh, yes. I've also been across the Rhine.

Of course! That's what I was talking about,
Places I've been . . . Salisbury! . . . when I had the gout.

Hurt like hell, but I just couldn't stop
Climbing those steps up to the very top.

That glorious Magna Charta was there.
It's not that anyone any longer really cares,

Not the Republicans, not Democrats, not anyone I know.
They'd just as soon vote for a pair of stilettos,

The guys for some sweet chick, in those pointed shoes,
Gals for the leather wrapped 'round their feet in blue.

Makes no difference what anyone thinks.
Can they smile, please the ear? It stinks!

What's this place come to? Blue! Red and white?
Forget the Native American. He lost the fight.

Am I making any sense, any sense at all?
I'll tell you this. There're times I'd like to just caterwaul

My way to the grave. There's that theme again.
Happens to all I guess, maybe 'specially men

When they reach my age, and then . . .
A word keeps running at them, "Amen, Amen."

It's over, this extraordinary life.
Just like you've been cut through with a rusty knife.

Makes no sense that we have to go
From where God put us so long ago.

Eden it ain't, but it ain't quite Gehenna.
Lost you, haven't I? Let me continue:

Salisbury's a place that comes close to Eden
Almost without a smidge of antecedence.

Thatched roofs grow everywhere you look.
I'd swear at each house there's a little brook

Running quietly along. Gives some kind of peace
To this sweet world. And, then there's Greece.

Been there, too, by the Aegean Sea
Out of which jumps flying trochee.

Poets galore raise their voices to the sky.
And I must admit, in my time, so did I.

Anapest, caesurae, dactyls, and damn!
I've forgotten the others. Like a magpie gone, and . . .

What were we talking about? Tell me again.
I've still got some of that good, sloe gin—

Okay, I've tried enough to get you drunk.
You've seen me before, do you think I've shrunk?

I get that over and over, well, now and then
Pisses me off that I've grown so thin.

Just yesterday morning, 'bout five a.m.,
I was walking the streets, ran into Jim,

Jim Porter, I mean.
He's the playwright. They call him the Dean.

Dean of *what?* A little play's not that hard.
Just throw in some dialogue with a bit of discord

And you've got it. Block some actors here and there.
What kind of game is that? "Adjust the mouth into a sneer."

See, don't have to do that in a poem you write.
You just have to prove that you're erudite

Like T. S. Eliot with that damned "Wasteland."
Talk about a waste, don't think anyone understands

What he was saying, 'cept his precious, intellectual few.
Now that would be a real, I mean real interview.

T. S. Eliot, poet and painter,
He'd give your readers 'bout the right amount of anger.

All his pomp and great affairs?
No question, he knew how to put on the aires.

If you're writing this down, too, I spell aire with an "e,"
Gives an effete feel Eliot deserves, from this old debauchee.

I mentioned Salisbury and the grand time we had there.
I don't think I mentioned the grand state of Delaware.

. . . Oh, yes. That's one of the "mis-states" I guess I missed.
Not sure how I could have been so remiss

As to let that place get by me.
Perhaps 'cause it's no larger than a flea

In the grand scale of things.
I hear it's quite extraordinary in the Spring.

But I've managed to digress again.
I've been to London, of course, seen Big Ben.

And I saw Vanessa Redgrave play Prosper.
Stood with the groundlings, could touch her toe

In the Old Globe Theatre, there on the Thames.
Did I mention I saw that tower of a clock, Big Ben?

What time is it now, close to lunch?
Could get you cheese and crackers, and some spiked punch.

No? Then, do you mind if I take a quick nap?
By the way, do you like all this damned rap?

Ahh, I know I'm all over the place,
A good power nap, then we can retrace

All the steps we've taken today.
Got a cot over there, you know what they say . . .

Fifteen minutes, probably no more.
I think I'm just gonna sleep right here on the floor.

Does my back good, right down there in the small.
But, I think I could use some rubbing alcohol.

Fifteen minutes, not one minute more.
No time even for one good snore.

Won't take me up on my little offer?
Puts a little change in the old body's coffer.

Okay, I'm gone, won't take me long
'Sides, I'll hear my ole clock gong.

Read in that book over there, or magazine,
Or if you want, some crackers and sardines?

Won't be long, just a little nappy-pooh.
Bid you a fond fifteen-minute adieu.

* * *

One minute over. Hey, not that bad.
Ready now to go again! Got more to add

About my lovely ole London, of course.
Besides *The Tempest*, saw *Henry the Fourth*,

King Lear and Yasmina Reza's *Art*.
If I saw 'em now, probably couldn't tell 'em apart.

I've written lots of poems over the years,
But plays like *Henry the Fourth*, Hear! Hear!

Part Two's the one I got to see.
Wanted to see Part One, that was on the marquee,

Or so I thought, so much for good eyesight.
Was that you just sneezed? Well, happy *Gesundheit*!

Now, Germany! What a lovely place to be or not have been,
Little *Hamlet* play on words there. Still got sloe gin.

You don't drink much for a big, fat guy.
By now, you oughta be *big* bone dry.

Okay, I promise. Won't ask again.
You know, don't have a clue 'bout where to begin

To talk about East Germany, that's where we went
Just as the wall was coming down—some enlightenment

There! Taxi cab driver in West Berlin
Was thrown into an absolute, complete tailspin

When I asked him in my very halting German
If he knew the way to East Berlin, and that simpleton

Said, "It's East of here's what I'd say."
Then, I realized that he wanted to play

With this American tourist whose German was weak.
Shit, for all he knew, I was speaking Greek.

Am I answering the question you asked earlier today?
You're satisfied? Well, I don't want to delay

That deadline your editor turd gave you.
If I went the wrong direction, you'd be screwed,

But that's the publishing business today,
It's died, curled up, and begun to decay

Like an armadillo in the middle of the road
Or a rattler, or rabbit, or maybe a toad.

I've hit 'em all at one time or another,
Can smell to high heaven, I mean Motha . . .

Sorry, I don't cuss much. Just not my way.
Not sure where that came from this time a day.

Well, there's really no time of day for that kind of thing.
Some folks just seem to need to vent their spleens.

See? Those last two lines would make a rhyme
In Texas almost all the time,

'Specially East Texas, that's where my wife came from.
West Texas is where you find all the petroleum

And lots of hot air that blows up the dust.
Now, just doesn't blow, gust after gust.

It blows all the time, never still day or night.
Ever seen one of those swirling wind sprites?

I'm sorry. I think I'd better go piss.
Your bladder's not something you can afford to dismiss

When you're ninety-three, going on ninety-four,
Don't worry. I know to shut the door.

Be right back, so don't go away.
I'm sorry 'bout the way my mind strays

Here and there and everywhere. Sorry 'bout that. This damned old age.
Wish they'd learn how to put a gauge

On this tired old bladder of mine.
Well, I don't really have all that much time

Left, so guess I shouldn't worry about it a lot.
Better than having the running trots.

What were we talking about? My pants'll dry.
Oh, yeah. Where've I been. Never been to Shanghai.

Never been farther east than way down under.
I'll tell you New Zealand is quite a wonder.

Felt like I has thrown back to the 1940's.
Got close to the South Pole, talk about freeze!

Watched those waddling penguins walk up the shore,
Thousands of Charlie Chaplins, no! Much, much more.

One of the cutest sights I ever did see.
I'm sorry, I think I've gotta go pee,

Again. Who knows how many times today.
I'll try to make it this time, so stay

Right where you are. Be right back.
Hey! How'd you like some nice French cognac?

Can't talk you into that one either?
Alright. Teetotaller. No? Me neither.

Sit right there. Make yourself at home.
When I get back, I'll tell you all I know about Rome.

* * *

Now, Rome! You thought I'd forget the spot
I was talking about. Thought of it on the pot.

Rome's the most exhilarating of places.
There's where you can see those famous Roman faces

With noses the length of a Caesar's gown
And complexions the most beautiful light brown.

I've never been more captured by a place I've been.
I can assure you I'd be a most willing citizen

Of *Roma*, with all its wonderful wines
And the countryside with green vines upon vines.

I taught in Rome in 1984,
Lived in a garret, caught up in all the lore
Of both the ancient and the modern city,
Romulus, Remus, Bacchus, and Mussolini.

The report was that just a few yards past my garret
Mussolini, with his henchmen, entertained some errant

Ladies of the night, night after night.
I walked to the ruins of the place in bright moonlight.

Story was the Americans thought they had him caught,
But you know American Intelligence, they just thought

They had him by the nape of the neck.
I'm getting hungry for an afternoon snack.

How 'bout you? Something to eat?
Oh, that reminds me of my island, Crete.

Had the worst calamari on the face of the earth.
Chewed, chewed, then chewed some more. Dessert

Was all I could think of, some nice Cretan cake.
Made by some cretin alright! Nothing but fake

Whipped cream on top of uncooked dough,
Wanted to rage my way into the kitchen and overthrow

The whole of the attending staff,
But my wife, well, she convinced me to laugh

It off as one bad choice on an otherwise great trip.
Next day I came down with a case of the grippe.

Now, I can't be sure the connection is right,
But I know I puked and puked and puked all night.

There was something big I was thinking about Crete.
Aah, yes! Those early Minoan athletes
Who catapulted over the heads of bulls.
The sight must have been beyond beautiful.

Men, women, too, I think
Flipping over bulls' heads in a wink,

Dressed in nothing or at most just thongs
While thousands cheered, throngs

Of women, children, men—young and old
Festooned in brilliant colors, red and gold

Worshipping Minos, son of Europa and Zeus.
you know, I've never been to Syracuse.

Have wanted to for years and years,
On the southeast cost of Sicily, water so clear

They say you can see your inner-soul
Reflected to you as from a silver bowl.

Haven't I taken enough of your time?
I think I just heard the clock in the bedroom chime.

What is it now, three o'clock?
Have I mentioned how much I love Johann Sebastian Bach?

Had a German Shepherd once, that's the name I gave him.
The lights in that dog's head were rather dim,

But I loved his addle-brained antics.
His leaps at the fence drove the postman into frantics.

Funny the things you remember at my old age,
Still, I can't remember my lines when I get on stage.

I did some acting. I told you, I suppose.
Dressed up in tights with long red hose.

Quite a sight, funny to me now,
But I'll never forget playing King Arthur, somehow.

Vanity of the actor, the writer, the man
In old age, willing to play any part, even Pan

To get attention or get a laugh.
Now, tell you who I'd like to play, Falstaff!

What a figure! Sack in his tunic and a chicken leg
With a belly that looks like an old ale keg.

I like the old guy. I'm right for the part,
On my right and left arm, a tart.

Those were the days. I'd go back there in a sec.
When I think of it, and I do think of it, oh, heck!

I'd go almost any place to get away from here,
I mean my decrepit age. I'd even play Lear.

I've told you about as much as I can, I think.
Imagine your pen's about to run out of ink.

Still need more, huh? How 'bout Casablanca for starts?
You know, northwest seaport in Morocco's heart.

I can't even say the name without thinking Bogart.
And, don't forget that loveliest of ladies, his sweetheart

Ingrid Bergman. I often throw myself back in time
To the big screen at the Bijou, a little slime and crime.

Bogart was a *real* man, or at least he played the part.
Sure grabbed my old girlfriends' hearts.

Hat cocked to the side and just a slight grin.
Don't suppose anyone was thought more masculine

Than Bogart, that short, smashed face of a man
Who always seemed to have the right plan

To deal with anything that came his way
In Casablanca, on a river, or in Calais.

You know, I've never been to France, least not yet.
Been to Normandy, saw the crosses and a long, low parapet

With azaleas blooming in honor of the dead.
Our world can be a place of dread, so much bloodshed.

I'll die, probably, in my bed asleep.
Or, if lucky in someone else's. Ha! Hope she's cheap.

I haven't got much money. Writers don't make much.
Shit! If we did anything, we'd have to go Dutch.

Oh, that reminds me. I've been to the Netherlands, too.

Actually, my home, Leerdam, Holland. Sky so blue

You'd think you'd fallen into a bottle of ink
The bluest of blues with streaks of sunset pink.

I felt right at home, spoke a little German,
Was absolutely bent to determine

If I could find a family member or so,
But everyone I asked simply said, "No,

We know absolutely no one by that name.
Sorry, so sorry, it's such a shame

That we're of so little assistance.
But, we'd say, don't give up. Be persistent.

There can't be too very many by the name Barent.
We assume that you've found that most apparent.

Keep looking is all that we would say.
If we were you, we'd take a sachet

To Amsterdam, only about seventy meters."
I went there but didn't find a Barent either.

I did find some very interesting things:
Young women in windows wearing lots of bling

And nothing else as I can best remember.
But keep in mind, this was in December.

Bling *is* the word, is it not, used today?
What you'd expect to see in Saint-Tropcz.

I like the word, sounds onomatopoetic.
Think I could make up quite a limerick.

Not sure exactly what I'd say,
But it would definitely include St. Vincent-Millay.

I can see ole Edna in one of those windows
Wearing red, with bling, and six-inch stilettos.

The cold wouldn't bother that ole broad.
Born in Maine where nothing thaws.

She was bi-sexual, I guess you know.
I haven't had sex with either, just too slow

In getting it up either morning or night.
It's a helluva, helluva, damnable plight.

But, who's gonna want an old guy like me?
I'm pushing for the big ole ninety-three.

No, think I told you earlier, I'm already there.
Have you noticed the big truancy in the back of my hair?

Not really truant, I guess, since it won't ever come back.
Some say a bald spot's an aphrodisiac

For women in old folks' homes, walking the floor.
I can't abide the thought of some old whore

Looking at my backside and sayin', "Oh, yeah.
He's for me. He's the cat's meow."

Got off the subject, didn't I?
Mind just flits along like some big magpie.

Have I mentioned Rome? I just don't remember.
My God, I don't know if it's May or November

Or June or July . . . what are the other months?
See, the head just does these horrible stunts.

Well, Rome, whether I mentioned it or not,
I think about Rome a lot. I mean a lot.

One of my favorite places in all the world.
It's a city that looks like an ancient pearl.

It's grimy, I know. Earthy, raw, full of spice.
Now, let me give you some very good advice:

Go to the catacombs, danker than Hell!

When you walk those corridors, you smell

Old, old death, where early Christians met, we're told.
Deep underground and acrid, biting cold.

I know. Why would anyone want to go there?
Well, I think because it leaves everything bare.

This is what it comes to, when life is gone:
Tombs in a wall. Life's one long marathon,

At least for me. And, I think of that often.
And, then, I think of a bright, shiny coffin

Stuck in the ground, like Christians in a wall.
Hey, I think this discussion needs some alcohol.

You say you'll finally take a drink?
Good, I know these ideas of mine stink

To high heaven. Now, there's a thought!
Heaven. Not sure whether I believe it or not.

Seems too pie in the sky for my theological taste.
I wonder how much time people spend, people waste

On thinking about heaven instead of this earth.
Too much, I know. It just isn't worth

The time people let flit away, wondering what's in store
For the faithful or the perfidious. It's such a bore!

Carpe diem, I say, but I do believe in God.
I've written a lot about Him/Her/It, a ballade,

A sonnet or three, several two-act plays,
Some short stories, prose poems . . . Okay,

I forgot your drink. What'll it be?
Think you'd enjoy a Long Island Tea?

Good! Then that's what it is. Goes down well,
And I can assure you, you won't go to Hell

For drinking with a ninety-five year old guy.
There I go again. Got the age wrong, don't know why

I can't keep a thing like that very straight.
You know, I had some carciofi in Rome. I ate

Plate after plate. You know, of course, it's artichoke,
But I think of it now as an extraordinary Baroque

Delicacy, the way those Italian chefs prepare it.
Did you know Baroque means imperfect pearl? Shit!

Nothing imperfect about that lovely dish.
Its leaves stood up like fifty Roman obelisks.

They were made of delectable pearl's all I can say.
I ate them in my little restaurant on every Tuesday.

Just remembered, I've not mentioned the other down under.
I've been to, Australia. An absolute wonder:

High desert, Sydney and Melbourne
Kangaroos jumping like hot popcorn,

Not unlike this mind of mine.
I suppose I'm in a real state of decline,

But, I'll never give up my travel.
I don't care how much of this brain unravels.

Put me on a plane, and I'll go anywhere.
Just give me a good, comfortable chair

Near the john. That, I'm afraid, is a necessity.
I can see from the nod of your head that you agree.

Was that the travel or the john?
Oh! You, too. An invitation and you're gone!

Well, then, let me tell you a bit more.
Turkey's surely not going to bore

You, neither Istanbul nor Kusadasi.
In Istanbul, wife and I went on a spending spree.

Bought two rather expensive prayer rugs.
We were locked in a room with a bunch of thugs

Who plied us with Turkish coffee and booze,
Laid before us rug upon rug and asked us to choose

Which ones we wanted. Like fools, we bought two.
For all we knew, they could have been made in Timbuktu.

But I thought my wife wanted one. She thought it was I.
So we bought two and said goodbye,

Walked out on the streets and could hear the wail
Of an Imam from atop a minaret. Sounded like travail,

But, it was beautiful to this Westerner's ears,
Not sure I've ever heard a voice so clear.

It climbed to the clouds, then leapt right through,
Then stopped. Sheer silence. Then started anew.

I'll never forget that splendid, foreign sound.
It danced through the sky, around and around.

It followed us all the way down to Kusadasi,
This once wondrous seaport by the Aegean Sea.

It had been ancient Ephesus, now beautifully restored.
None of my travels has given such reward

To a professor, writer, and reader of ancient times.
I left our guide, almost ran far ahead, and climbed

Through the rocks and the marble and the bright porticos.
I might have even struck a Biblical pose

By the magnificent library façade.
My wife told me the guide said, "That's odd!

I don't see the professor. Has he gotten lost?"
I was sitting on some steps thinking of Pentecost.

Not that the Biblical tale took place there.
But, somehow it all just permeated air

That surrounded this stunning archeological dig.
I felt like dancing some St. Pauline jig.

I've been to the state of Israel, too,
And I can't even begin to tell you whose

History (feigned or real) struck me most behind the eyes.
I think of it now, and I want to cry

With sadness and with joy. Sadness for the plight of Jews,
Joy for the energy of Israel. Is this really an interview?

I've done nothing but talk and talk and talk.
Think you'd like to take a little walk

Down the street to my favorite pub?
Interesting name: *Beelzebub*.

It's been thought that this was the god known as Ba'al.
We could go get a nice dark ale.

By now you know I'm a universalist.
Actually was once called a Communist

By some older people who resisted change.
To this very day I find that strange:

Why must the *world* be so damned stiff
In its beliefs about this and that. It's as if

We thought we knew everything to be known.
And on and on and on we drone

About Truth, as though we were certain we know.
We know nothing! Our minds are so slow

They wrestle with the simplest of things.
If I could give my knowledge grand, wide wings

I'd still not fly above the top of this table.
None of us, not a single one of us is able

To be so damned certain of this or of that.
No more sense than a Tasmanian wombat.

We believe! And, that's all we can do.
Christian, Sikh, Muslim, or Jew . . .

We *all* believe, it's what's called "faith."
And, if we want to talk about that pearly gate,

I believe (don't *know*) that we're all just stumblers,
Moving toward a god . . . yes, bumblers

Who do the very best that we can
Over some ninety-plus-year span . . .

Oh, what is the right word?
I feel, right now, like your editor turd

Must feel with a bright red pen in hand
In her great editorial Holy Land.

You see I sometimes reach for words,
Might as well be playing a clavichord

Which I've never played even once in my life.
My head's so miserably swirling round and rife

With first this and then again that.
It rushes along, night and day, a crazed bat.

So, I try to sit still for a moment or so
And hope I'll still this imbroglio

In this old head. Times are getting very tough.
At times I feel like Shakespeare's McDuff.

You remember, I'm sure, the one who killed Macbeth.
The whole play's about, what else? Death.

I think I'm dying. Should be no surprise.
We should probably hurry and summarize

All I've said for that editor of yours.
Want to be certain, keep your job secure.

Forgot to say I've been to the Isle of Patmos
Hallucinating John must have gone comatose.

I mean, apocalyptic beasts and all those things?
Sounds like he botched up his clock's mainspring.

I went into the cave where he conjured all of this.
And everything he wrote seems an antithesis

To writings like the Sermon on the Mount
Now, that is writing! Writing absolutely paramount

From this writer's point of view.
Same John who wrote both? Don't have a clue.

But, the point I was making . . . been right there.
Didn't see four horsemen, looked for horsehair,

But all I saw was rock and sublime sea.
Enough to satisfy my proclivity

For all things beautiful in this extraordinary world.
Waves crashing in ashore, whitecaps pearled

Beyond my imagination.
But, then, I'm something of a simpleton.

Had enough, my patient friend?
I have many, many more places to recommend,

But I'd guess you've had 'bout enough.
There's Delphi, Epidaurus, and all that stuff.

But, I'm getting tired. Eyes heavy, thoughts slow.
Let me tie all this up in a nice sweet bow.

Writers tend to do that. I hate it with a passion.
But, it's become the bad writer's fashion.

I've been lots of places, most with my wife.
I can say, without question, I've had quite a life.

The question I've addressed is not what you wanted.
Gotta admit, when I heard it, I punted.

Well, kicked the ball as far as *I* could.
Mighta spent hours on hours and just spewed

It out: "Where am I?" You *meant* my writing, of course.
I knew all along, but no writer wants to give discourse

On what he or she's writing or written.
Except those writers entirely smitten

With their own words who must hear their ejaculations.
Yeah, ejaculations. That's what I said. Word permutations.

That say nothing, nothing at least you wanta hear.
They spout off with deep voices, sound like King Lear.

For me, I write what I write and then it's yours.
Call it glorious, call it sick. Call it plain amateur.

I could care less. I've done it because I needed to write.
I'm really not trying to be impolite.

I'm just tired, said all I need to say.
What day this? Is it Saturday?

Seven o'clock? That's past my bedtime.
Goin' to bed. Hope you get to hear Big Ben chime.

As for me, well, at ninety-three,
There's not much more for me to see.

Close the door when you leave the house.
When you spell my name, it's with an umlaut.

Ha, I'll look in the obituary, in the a.m.
Be sure and give me a stately requiem.

Brahms-like would be quite, quite nice.
But, don't misunderstand. Don't eulogize.

I want some ragtime, some blues, or a dance.
To make me forget I didn't see France.

Four Horsemen of the Apocalypse

Ambiguity

Once, as a boy of five
or six, I named the colors
of a sunrise. "Red and blue,"
I said. But I was just a child,
and all things in the world
needed and could be given names.

Today, some sixty or so years past
innocence, the sun rose again
(it always does, or so I must inductively
assume) but not in childlike, nomenclature hues.
It rose with slow, rich, ambiguous complications
and could no more be named
than can the act of making love.

And so for tomorrow, and other sunrises
to come, ask me for no colors.
That is not a sensible request,
nor will I be inclined to answer
as I shall be engaged busily in nameless
acts of lovemaking with the sky.

Colors of the Spirit

Laughter

    —for Mary

Like alchemists of old
we hammered worthless metal into gold
slipped circles on our young fingers
and knew the fitting would linger

past the power of intrusions,
even subtle nibbling frictions.
You would follow me, I follow you
until each would need help to do

what so happily, so freely, had been done before:
walk apace, even run together, play tennis,
though you never really did. We still laugh
at our aging blunders and inabilities.

Is that not what the world was made for?
Laughter? Our world *still* turns and
laughs, too, I would suppose, at our
forgetting close friends, names, last

street addresses, and that favorite author's
name—even that this earth is actually circling
the moon. Surely we won't forget the moon
we walked under in '52.

Bright yellows and whites, partially hidden
by the blowing sands of West Texas.
It was ours, only ours, and will be
even beyond laughter and forgetting.

Feet

I have been asked to write a poem about my feet. I believe it was God who asked. Not certain, one of those sleepless nights. The voice carried a voice quality, not unlike a PBS announcer's. Certainly not sharp or commanding, simply, "Take your shoes off. Admire your exquisite feet."

I did, but very slowly, as I've never thought my feet exquisite, only bony with very little flab on them (wonder what the etymology of that word is). Ahh! Looked it up: from the Old French indicating "soft" and "limp." Interesting, I ordinarily think of other body parts to satisfy that

definition. Feeling like the Gentile version of the Jewish Wanderer, my feet feel crusty, dry. It seems I've travelled thousands of miles in life, not for some penance to be paid as in the Wanderer of Wanderers. Feet ache, burn, and are clearly the first parts of my God-made body to go.

Call it peripheral neuropathy if you wish, I don't care. They just take glee in shooting pains up through my wisdom teeth which are still all there. I now throb from head to feet, or feet to head. You don't care, do you? I understand that. It's my sole(s) to bear. And, I will . . . because

there are roads yet to walk, whatever the pain, so many things yet to see, so much yet to do. Exquisite feet, put me in never-ending motion.

Three Is Company

Breaking Conformity's Back

Afterword

This collection of my poems and paintings seems almost like a lifelong work, though I have many more poems and paintings than you see here. And, there will be many more to come in my future, should all go as planned. However, what ever does? My shifting mind is filled with more ideas than this (my 5th book of poetry) or any future books might hold, flitting about somewhat as they must have in the mind of Don Quixote. So, I may return to one of my other great loves, for now, playwriting or another, the short story.

Interestingly, my wife has called me Don Quixote for many years of our marriage. I'm hopeful she's meaning Quixote's idealism and not his quirkiness, though I've been correctly charged with that, as well. *Quixotic Notions* had its real beginning in 2011, though I didn't know it at the time. This was the year I began digital painting, just playing to see what I could do following a few years of watercolors. My poetry had begun in graduate school, and at some juncture I began thinking about bringing my two art forms together, my poems and my new love, digital paintings.

I must thank Dr. Jerry Craven for the windfall of this book. He contacted me, saying that he'd like to have one of my books for the Lamar University Literary Press. I told him I would be glad to send one on, and his surprising comment to me was that he meant he wanted to do a new book with me, an unusual book. And, it's that unusual book that you may be holding in your hands. My searching mind is attached to so many different ideas: the many beauties of our world, the sorrows...even threats. This is a collection of many rather than a singular dancing theme.

How remiss I would be if I didn't give credit to my wife, Mary. She's suffered the cluttered writer's garret (my bedroom in which I never placed my head on a pillow at all, some nights). And, no one could have ever been so patient as she with the consuming time I have taken with my graduate students in seminars and required individual meetings, my writing, and painting. She is the love of many years, as are my students. I have a family of great ones at S.M.U: poets and writers of fiction who have made me enormously proud of their own publications, quite a number of them... and pleased, most of all for all I have learned from every one of them. I believe, when this publication reaches them, I'll begin to call each, individually, my ever-so-wise and talented Pancho. Rich, rich words for my Editor, Katie Hoerth, and Associate Editor, Theresa L Ener.

Last words from my favorite poet: Rainer Maria Rilke

"For one human being to love another; that is perhaps the most difficult of all our tasks, the ultimate, the last test and proof, the work for which all other work is but preparation. Love consists in this, that two solitudes protect and touch and greet each other."